THE WASHINGTON PAPERS
Volume IV

39: Saudi Arabia

David E. Long

THE CENTER FOR STRATEGIC AND INTERNATIONAL STUDIES
Georgetown University, Washington, D.C.

SAGE PUBLICATIONS
Beverly Hills / London

Printed in the United States of America

For information address:

SAGE PUBLICATIONS, INC.
275 South Beverly Drive
Beverly Hills, California 90212

SAGE PUBLICATIONS LTD
28 Banner Street
London EC1Y 8QE, England

International Standard Book Number 0-8039-0660-9

Library of Congress Catalog Card No. 76-49790

THIRD PRINTING

When citing a Washington Paper, please use the proper form. Remember to cite the series title and include the paper number. One of the two following formats can be adapted (depending on the style manual used):

(1) HASSNER, P. (1973) "Europe in the Age of Negotiation." The Washington Papers, I, 8. Beverly Hills and London: Sage Pubns.

OR

(2) Hassner, Pierre. 1973. *Europe in the Age of Negotiation.* The Washington Papers, vol. 1, no. 8. Beverly Hills and London: Sage Publications.

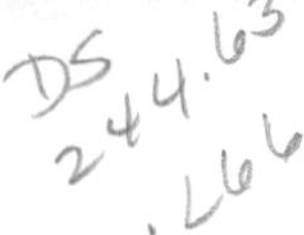

he desert, but temperatures drop rapidly at sunset in the dry air. long the coasts, the high humidity militates against such ex-remes, but summers are quite oppressive with temperatures overing around 100 to 115 degrees Farenheit and the humidity the high 90s.

In elevation, Saudi Arabia is shaped like a giant playing card, pped up on its western, or Red Sea side. Alongside the Red Sea nd extending inland 15 to 75 miles is a hot, desolate coastal lain known as Tihama. It is occasionally traversed by dry river alleys or *wadis,* originating in the mountains to the east. These adis provide sufficient underground water and occasional runoff ater from infrequent rains to support limited agriculture. The rgest city in Tihama is Jiddah, a commercial center for the ntire kingdom and the gateway to Mecca, the holiest city in lam. Mecca is about 50 miles to the east, surrounded by barren ocky hills but still well within the coastal plain. A few miles east f Mecca is the plain of Arafat where over 1,500,000 Muslims ather annually to celebrate the Hajj or Great Pilgrimage, required f each Muslim at least once during his lifetime if he is physically nd financially able to make the trip.

Rising abruptly from the plain is a relatively narrow escarp-ent running the entire length of Saudi Arabia. Altitudes vary om 3,000 to 4,000 feet in the north and reach 10,000 feet in e south. In neighboring Yemen, further to the south, the ountains exceed heights of 12,000 feet.

The northern segment of the mountains and plain form the ijaz, once an independent kingdom. Its most important cities ter Mecca and Jiddah are al-Madinah, the second most holy city Islam, located about 275 miles to the north, and al-Taif, just st of Mecca. Al-Taif, with an elevation of nearly 6,000 feet, is metimes considered the winter capital of Saudi Arabia.

The region south of al-Taif is called Asir. Its regional capital is bha, 8,000 feet up in the mountains. Nearby on the coast is the aport town of Jizan, connected to Abha by a new road which imbs the escarpment in a series of hair-raising switchback rves, just as the Mecca-al-Taif road does farther north. South-st of Abha is the Wadi Najran, a fertile dry-river valley and land gateway between Saudi Arabia and the Yemen.

CONTENTS

Dedicated to my wife Barbara

PREFACE

Saudi Arabia has become almost a household word in the wake of the energy crisis and the Arab embargo of 1973-1974. As the world's greatest oil exporter and possessor of the largest proved oil reserves, its petroleum and investment policies have become a major factor in the world economy. Its new economic power, when translated into political power, has added a new dimension to the nearly thirty-year-old Arab-Israeli dispute.

Much has been published about the implications of Saudi Arabia's new role in the Free World economy and in Middle East politics. At the same time, very little has been written of Saudi Arabia itself. For example, nowhere since Philby's *Arabian Jubilee* (1953) has there appeared a current geneology of the royal family. This brief study is designed as an introduction to acquaint the reader with Saudi Arabia's social and economic structure and its political dynamics. Only by understanding these factors can we develop an adequate basis for evaluating the plethora of topical analysis on the implications of Saudi policies.

I should like to express my appreciation to all those whose valued assistance and suggestions went into the study, particularly Graeme Bannerman and Nizar al Madani who read the manuscript, Mona Jallad who typed it, and my wife Barbara who proofread it.

–D.L.E.

I. THE ENVIRONMENT

Saudi Arabia is a land of contrasts. A huge co sparsely populated. A barren land, it is endow world's largest proved oil reserves. It is a land where conservative and traditional way of life is challen impact of oil-financed Western technological chan anywhere one turns in studying Saudi Arabia, one anomaly.

The Land

Saudi Arabia has a land area of approximately 830, miles,[1] equivalent to the United States east of the minus New England. The country extends approxima miles from north to south and 1,000 miles from east to farthest extremities.

Although nearly all Saudi Arabia is hot and dry, ther variations in climate. Winters are generally balmy, but be quite cold in the mountains and interior. It is p experience subfreezing temperatures at night during t ummers are very hot and have reached 140 degrees Fa

The Asir is the only part of Saudi Arabia to receive regular rainfall, from Indian Ocean monsoons. Its terrain, terraced fields, and stone-built villages, are more reminiscent of the Yemen or of Lebanon than the rest of Saudi Arabia. It even boasts several perennial streams. Rainfall can be undependable, however, and it is not uncommon for the region to experience droughts of several years duration.

East of the mountains, the terrain slopes away gradually until it reaches sea level along the shores of the Persian Gulf. Central Arabia is called Najd. Its most prominent land feature is Jabal Tuwaiq, a westward facing escarpment which extends 600 miles in a shallow arc from north to south. The major population center of Najd is Riyadh, the capital. In a generation it has grown from an isolated mud brick oasis town to a city of skyscrapers and auto-choked streets. Northwest of Riyadh in the Qasim district are the rival major towns of Anayzah and Buraydah. Beyond them in the Jabal Shammar district, lies the town of al-Hayil, seat of the Al Rashids, historic rivals of the House of Saud. Southwest of Riyadh is the oasis of al-Kharj, a major military center.

Along the Persian Gulf coast lies the Eastern Province. A low, barren plain dotted with rocky outcrops, its chief population centers are the vast Hasa (al-Ahsa) Oasis with its principal town Hufuf, and the smaller Qatif Oasis. Hasa once gave its name to the entire area, but with the coming of oil, Dhahran is now better known. It comes as a surprise to many first time visitors to the Eastern Province that Dhahran is not really a Saudi town at all. It is the collective name for the relatively scattered Arabian American Oil Company (ARAMCO) headquarters and residential area, the Petroleum and Minerals University campus, the American consulate general compound, and the Dhahran airport complex. The two population centers in the vicinity are Dammam, the capital of the Eastern Province, and al-Khubar, south of Dammam and east of Dhahran. North of Dammam, past the Qatif Oasis is Ras Tanura, the site of Saudi Arabia's major oil refinery and loading terminal. About 25 miles east southeast of al-Khubar and visible on a clear night is the island archipelago of Bahrain, out in the Persian Gulf.

In the south of Saudi Arabia, one enters the vast, trackless Rub' al-Khali, the Empty Quarter. Stretching for 250,000 square miles (about the size of Texas), it is the largest sand desert in the world. Its distinctive pink sand dunes rise to a height of 800 feet. The few Bedouin tribes who traverse this forbidding place call it merely "the sands." In more recent years, however, oil has been discovered in the eastern reaches of the Empty Quarter, giving it a new economic importance.

Najd, central Arabia, is surrounded on three sides by deserts of pink sand. In the north, the Great Nafud, though smaller than the Rub' al-Khali, presents a formidable barrier to overland travel. Moreover, it extends southward in a continuous strip to the Rub'al-Khali. This strip of dunes, called the Dahna, separates Najd from the Eastern Province.

Because of its importance as a major oil producer, the geology of Saudi Arabia is of as much interest as its terrain. Most of Saudi Arabia is situated in a huge sedimentary basin extending from the Anatolian highlands of Turkey to the Hajar Mountains of Oman, and from the Hijaz Mountains in the west to the Zagros Mountains of Iran in the east.

The Hijaz Mountains are volcanic in origin and geologically are a part of a pre-Cambrian shield or basement complex, one of the oldest formations known. To the east, the geology, though ancient, is of more recent origin than the Hijaz. The waters of the Persian Gulf at one time covered this area and sedimentary marine deposits accumulated on top of the basement complex. Over time, this great sedimentary basin began to sink gently toward the east and the fossilized remains of marine life were gradually transformed into oil deposits, caught in pockets in the limestone and sandstone rock strata. These pockets, known as domes or anticlines, are the present day oil fields.

There has been some exploration for other minerals in Saudi Arabia but no discoveries have been made which even approach its oil resources. In the Wadi Sirhan, acquired from Jordan in an adjustment of the Saudi-Jordanian border some years ago, there are known phosphate deposits. They were originally not thought to be commercially marketable but the rise in the world price of phosphates may make them so.

Hijazi society is also less conservative than Najdi society. Hijazi sons have not only had more contact with the outside world, but traditionally have had more broadly based educations than Najdis, and have produced many of the country's leading bureaucrats and technocrats. Political power, however, remains firmly in the hands of the Najdis. This has made some Hijazis impatient, thinking themselves more sophisticated and better administrators. Hijazis, on the other hand, were traditionally considered to be politically suspect by Najdis who conquered the Hijaz in 1926, deposing the ruling Hashimite House, still in power in Jordan. In more recent years, however, with the great strides in nationwide economic and social development, Nadji-Hijazi rivalry has slackened considerably.

It is more difficult to get a feel for the "personality" of the Eastern Province than for the other of Saudi Arabia's regions. Historically, two oases—al-Hasa and al-Oatif—comprised the major population centers. The oasis dwellers were mainly date farmers, though on the coast, fishing, sea faring and pearl diving were also important. As elsewhere on the Persian Gulf coast, there was a sizeable minority of Shi'ah Muslims, and contact with Iran and the East gave the area an outlook different from the rest of the country.

The coming of oil has greatly changed the character of the Eastern Province, but in ways that are difficult to define with any precision. The oil industry has drawn Saudis from every corner of the kingdom, third-country Arabs, and nationals from Europe, America, Africa, and Asia as well. This polyglot of people conforms to Western work habits, working on regular shifts and drawing regular pay checks. In addition to the oil industry, which is primarily located in the Eastern Province, subsidiary service industries have also grown up there. With a relatively high, steady income, many workers own their own homes in Damman or al-Khubar and are thoroughly middle class in outlook.

Side by side with the modern economic sector, however, many of the oasis dwellers have resisted change and continue in their age-old pursuits. Tarut Island, near al-Qatif, for example, appears to be separated from the nearby refinery at Ras Tanura by at least 300 years. There is yet a third class, those who work in the modern sector by day and return to their villages by night.

The Eastern Province, in which is concentrated most of the nation's oil wealth, is ironically overshadowed politically and commercially by Najd and the Hijaz. Although it does boast several large merchant families, few are on a scale with those from Jiddah and Riyadh. Politically, the *amir* (governor) has always been a member of the Bin Jiluwi branch of the royal family. Few of the leading government bureaucrats in the area are actually native to the area. In sum, the Eastern Province is one of the most amorphous areas in Saudi Arabia.

By contrast, Asir is more homogeneous, due in part to its isolation. It is also one of the least known and most populous regions of the kingdom. Asiris, living in small mountain villages, are a hard-working, good-natured people. Less conservative than Najdis, their women seldom wear the veil. As new roads and airports open the region, however, great social changes are inevitable.

In the far north are several provinces whose populations are largely tribal in orientation. Tribes in this area roam from Saudi Arabia north to Jordan, Syria, and Iraq. Like the Najdis, they are desert aristocrats and from their number are recruited many of the tribally organized troops of the Saudi National Guard.

Social Development

In Saudi Arabia a traditional, conservative Islamic society has suddenly been confronted with the full force of twentieth century Western technology and thought. Despite the rapid social change, the impact of Islam on the culture and society of the Middle East—and particularly on Saudi Arabia—cannot be overstated. There is no separation of the sacred and the secular in Islam. More than a religion, it is an all-embracing way of life affecting Muslim and non-Muslim alike.

In Saudi Arabia, the constitution and legal system are based directly on Islamic or Shari'ah law; time is still computed by the sun, a system geared to the Muslim cycle of five prayers daily (a new "day" begins at sunset, the time of which varies each day). A lunar calendar is used because it marks the Muslim religious holidays, particularly the *Hajj;* a religious police force (the *Mutawa'iin*) enforces religious regulations; no public cinemas or alcohol are allowed and no non-Muslims are allowed in the holy cities of Mecca and al-Madinah. Even for one who is no longer a conscientious believer, the Saudi's perceptions of law, politics, ethics, and society—indeed his view of the world—have been indelibly and inescapably molded by Islam.

Because Islam teaches that God is the creator of all things and ultimately responsible for all actions, Saudis have been imbued with a profound sense of the inevitability of events. An often-heard phrase in Saudi Arabia is *inshallah*, or "if God wills it." For if God does not will it, no matter what the statistical probability, it simply cannot happen.

This feeling of inevitability is often labeled Muslim "fatalism". The term fatalism, however, connotes passivity, and Muslim fatalism is far from that. For example, Saudis share with other Arabs the conviction that inevitably they will succeed in the cause against Zionism, and it has never occurred to them passively to accept Israeli settlement terms, even in the face of defeat. Moreover, this feeling of inevitability is seldom consciously perceived. Rather, it is a subconscious view of the order of things. Thus, while at the conscious level, a Saudi can work with high proficiency in a technological milieu, it would be a mistake to assume that the transfer of Western technology and education have obliterated his acceptance of the inevitable.

Since God (or fate) rather than probability determines actions, Saudis feel less inclined than Westerners to make their behavior appear consistent; like Orientals, their thinking is compartmentalized. Thus, political, business, and personal relationships can be held separate, even at the cost of apparent inconsistency. For example, whereas Saudi Arabia refuses to have any political relations with a communist state, communist products are sold freely in its markets.

On the other hand, all relationships are highly personalized. It occasionally comes as a shock to Western businessmen that Saudis have rejected their product or service, clearly the most competitive, because of a disinclination to do business with the person representing the firm.

The impact of Western technology and thought on Saudi society is far more difficult to weigh. From the time of his accession to the throne in 1964, the late King Faysal had attempted to acquire for his people the material benefits of modern technology while maintaining the purity of Islamic society embodied in the Wahhabi religious revival.

Faysal's Ten Point Reform Program, first published in 1962, incorporated both social welfare and economic development. Subsequently, Saudi Arabia embarked on a five year economic development plan in 1970 and a second five year plan in 1975 with projected expenditures of $149 billion. Even if only a fraction of this is actually spent, it represents a staggering amount. Under King Khalid, more social welfare programs and even political reforms are expected. These programs have already transformed Saudi Arabia. Once an insular desert kingdom, it now plays an important part in both Middle East and indeed world politics.

Schools have been established throughout the country and education is free. During 1974-1975, 772,000 Saudi students were enrolled, of whom 616,000 were in elementary school, 104,000 in intermediate schools, and 28,000 in secondary schools. The preponderance of elementary school students is an indication of the rapidly expanding educational base in Saudi Arabia. In addition, in the same year there were 5,000 students in technical and vocational training schools and 19,000 university students. Three modern universities have been established in Saudi Arabia: The University of Petroleum and Minerals in Dhahran, Abd al-Aziz University in Jiddah, and al-Riyadh University in the capital. Several thousand students also are studying abroad for advanced degrees, over 3,000 in the United States alone.

The education of women, a revolutionary concept a generation ago, is now taken for granted. The changing role of women is itself an interesting study in Saudi Arabia. Traditionally, women were relegated strictly to the home and Saudi women still go veiled when they are in public. Moreover, social life was segregated by sex, a husband having his male circle of friends, and a wife her circle of friends among the women. Education and travel are beginning to modify these attitudes however. Manpower shortages are also creating pressure to bring more women into the labor force. It will probably not be very long before the veil, one of the most visible vestiges of the traditional way of life, begins to disappear.

On the other hand, there is one aspect of the traditional way of life which many Saudi women find hard to give up. Life in Saudi Arabia revolves around the extended family, with brothers, uncles, cousins, children, and their immediate families often living together in large housing compounds. In this milieu, home life is dominated by the women. If a husband has a quarrel with his wife, he must contend not only with her but with her sisters, his sisters, their aunts, their mothers, and if he has taken a second wife (a practice now largely dying out), she will generally side with the first wife against him. In short, although Saudi women are relegated to the home, they wield considerable power there.

In addition, because most Saudi social life is centered in the home and among the sexes, there would be little for a Saudi woman to do with Western style liberation were she to achieve it. She is already free to visit among her women friends as she wishes. It is primarily when she goes abroad that a Saudi woman can benefit from being free of the constraints of the traditional social system. Even then, however, some less out-going Saudi women look forward to returning to Saudi Arabia and the power they can exercise in the home.

Health care is free and new hospitals are being constructed. The new King Faysal Hospital in Riyadh is one of the most modern anywhere. Saudis are also sent abroad free of charge for medical services not obtainable in the country. A new all-weather road system links all but the remote areas, and the Saudi air service is excellent. Saudi Arabian Airlines is the largest carrier in the Middle East. Saudis of all classes board airplanes as casually as their grandfathers mounted camels, and even nomads have taken to driving from place to place. It is common to see a shiny new red pick-up truck beside a traditional goat hair tent.

Despite some initial opposition, King Faysal instituted public radio and television. Saudi Radio, offering domestic and foreign radio service, is operated by the Ministry of Information. Religiously oriented broadcasts are beamed from Radio Mecca, which is part of the network. The Saudi television network has studios in the major cities, including Qasim Province and al-Madinah. In order to win over the conservative religious leadership to the establishment of radio and television (and also as a mark of his own piety), Faysal had large portions of program time devoted to Qu'ran readings and religious instruction. The transistor radio of course had already brought the outside world to the farthermost reaches of the kingdom. Early radios were called "Ahmad Saids" by many of the Bedouins, after a colorful Cairo radio announcer of the day. It is estimated there are over one million radio receivers in Saudi Arabia, with an audience of some three million. There are also some 400,000 television sets, with an audience of around one million.

With the exception of the official gazette, *Umm al-Qura*, the Saudi press is privately owned. All newspapers, however, are subject to regulation by the Ministry of Information. The four largest Arabic daily papers—*al-Madinah, al-Ukaz, al-Nadwah*, and *al-Bilad*—are published in the Hijaz, as is the country's new English language daily, *Arab News*. The leading daily in the capital is *al-Riyadh*, although a Riyadh weekly, *al-Jizirah*, also plans to put out a daily edition. In the Eastern Province, the principal newspaper is *al-Yawm*.

Bookshops and newspaper stands are located in all the major towns and cities but selection is limited. With very little domestic publishing, most books and magazines are imported. As with the press, they are also subject to regulation by the Ministry of Information. The intention is not merely to monitor political content but also to insure against the distribution of reading materials which would be offensive in Saudi Arabia's conservative Islamic society.

With the introduction of all these modern elements, it is impossible to expect Saudi society not to be affected. It is very difficult, however, to judge Saudi public opinion in the present state of transition. Unlike many countries in the Middle East, there has been no perceptible influence on the population by leftist or radical ideologies. In the late 1960s a number of arrests for alleged political dissidence were made largely from the armed forces, but speculation that the arrests were symptomatic of a general current of political unrest proved to be unfounded. Perhaps the explanation for the stability that Saudi Arabia has enjoyed is the combination of a basically conservative society and the economic opportunities afforded by oil wealth, which serve to undermine the effectiveness of possible political dissatisfaction.

II. HISTORICAL BACKGROUND

Saudi Arabia is a new country in an old land. References to Arabia are as old as recorded history. Muslims, however, consider the founding of Islam in the early seventh century A.D. as the most important historical fact occurring in the Arabian Peninsula.[2] To Muslim historians all pre-Islamic history is labelled the "age of ignorance" *(jahiliyyah).* The modern Kingdom of Saudi Arabia, on the other hand, dates only from 1932 when it was created by King Abd al-Aziz bin Abd al-Rahman Al Saud, known in the West as "Ibn Saud."[3]

King Abd al-Aziz's forefathers had already ruled in Arabia for over 200 years, so that the history of Saudi Arabia is more precisely the history of the Al Saud, the royal family. The founder of the family, Muhammad bin Saud (c. 1703-1704-1792), was the hereditary ruler of a petty Najdi principality, Dir'iyyah. In the year 1744-1745, the Amir Muhammad became the patron of Shaykh Muhammad bin Abd al-Wahhab, a zealous religious revivalist from the neighboring town of Uyainah.[4]

Muhammad bin Abd al-Wahhab preached the return to the conservative interpretation of orthodox (*Sunni*) Islam as contained in the Hanbali school of Islamic jurisprudence, and as taught by a Syrian Hanbali writer, Ibn Taymiyah (1262-1328

A.D.)[5]. Specifically, he condemned practices which had grown up since Muhammad's day, such as revering saints and making pilgrimages to their tombs. Calling for a return to strict monotheism, he branded these practices as politheist and their adherents as non-Muslims. To this day, Wahhabis, as the followers of the revival are called,[6] bury their dead in unmarked graves in the desert lest the tomb of a revered person become a religious shrine.

The spiritual force of the Wahhabi revival led by the Al al-Shaykh (House of the Shaykh, as Abd al-Wahhab's descendents are called) when combined with the temporal power of the Al Saud proved irresistible. By the end of the century, nearly all of central Arabia had fallen under Saudi control.

As long as the rise of the Sauds and their Wahhabi followers was limited to central Arabia, it attracted little outside attention. In the early nineteenth century, however, Saudi control began to expand in all directions. In 1801 the Wahhabis sacked the town of Karbala in what is now southern Iraq and destroyed the domed tombs of various holy men, including the tomb of Muhammad's grandson, Husayn, venerated by Shi'ah Muslims. Indeed, Karbala is considered the most holy city after Mecca and al-Madinah in Shi'ah Islam.

In 1806, Wahhabi warriors seized Mecca and al-Madinah, defeating the Ottoman Turkish garrisons. In the east, Wahhabi armies pushed into Oman, and forced the Sultan in Muscat to pay tribute to the Saudi amirs. In the Persian Gulf, Arab privateers, newly converted to the revival, sailed forth to prey on the merchant ships of nonbelievers there and in the Indian Ocean. The British, who by then were the principal Western maritime power in the area, branded them pirates, and the lower Gulf coast was given the epithet, "Pirate Coast." From the point of view of the Wahhabi mariners, however, it was virtually a religious duty to make war upon the ships of Western unbelievers and non-Wahhabi Muslim "heretics" as well.

The rise of the Saudi state was so rapid, and adherence to the Wahhabi revival so compelling, that one can only speculate how far it might have expanded had it not met the superior military technology of its external opponents. After all, men such as these had spread the original doctrine of Islam from the Atlantic to the

Pacific, and from Asia to Africa and Europe. After their initial, spectacular successes, however, opposition to the Saudis crystallized. Shaken by the loss of Mecca and al-Madinah, the Ottoman Sultan asked his Egyptian Viceroy, Muhammad Ali, to recover the lost territories and invade Najd.

Muhammad Ali sent his son, Ibrahim Pasha, to Arabia to deal with the Wahhabis. After a bitter, seven year campaign, Ibrahim Pasha succeeded in capturing the Saudi capital at Dir'iyyah in 1818. The Saudi Amir, Abdallah ibn Saud Al Saud, fourth in line, was exiled to Cairo and later to Constantinople where he was subsequently beheaded. Dir'iyyah was razed and never recovered. Its ruins can still be seen along the Wadi Hanifah, north of the present capital, Riyadh.

With the collapse of the Saudi state, the Wahhabis in the Persian Gulf area were left largely to their own devices. The British had sent several expeditions to quell the "pirates" between 1805 and 1818, but without success. Then, in December 1819, a large British naval and land force gathered off Ras al-Khaymah. The resulting Arab defeat and subsequent treaty, signed in 1820, suppressed the privateers once and for all and set the stage for British hegemony in the Gulf for the next 150 years.

The years of Ottoman-Egyptian occupation, 1818-1822, were harsh. Ibrahim Pasha was less interested in consolidating political power than in destroying the political base of the Sauds so that they could never again threaten the holy cities of the Hijaz, Mecca, and al-Madinah. Not only was the capital, Dir'iyyah, destroyed and its palm groves cut down, but as many of the Al Saud and Al al-Shaykh as could be gathered up were exiled to Cairo.

By 1822, following the withdrawal of part of the Egyptian-Turkish garrisons, various local leaders raised the standard of revolt. The outstanding leader, Turki bin Abdallah Al Saud, was able to reassert Saudi control in the next year. Before his assassination in 1834, he had already consolidated all of the former Saudi territories except the Hijaz which was still under Ottoman control. He had also moved his capital to Riyadh.

Turki's son Faysal, who had been taken in exile to Cairo, escaped and returned to his father in 1827-1828. Following the death of his father, Faysal rose against the usurper, Mishari, and became the new Imam, sixth in the Saudi line.

In 1837, however, a cousin, Khalid, who was a brother of Abdallah, the last Imam of Dir'iyyah, rose in revolt. Khalid, little more than a puppet of Cairo, was aided by an Egyptian army. Faysal was captured in 1838 and again exiled to Cairo. But, with the Egyptian partial troop withdrawal in 1840, Khalid's fortunes waned quickly. After a desultory reign of just over four years, he was ousted in 1841 by Abdallah bin Thunayan, descended from a brother of a founder of the dynasty, Muhammad bin Saud. Abdallah reigned less than two years, for in the previous year Faysal had again escaped and by 1843 was for the second time undisputed ruler of Najd.

Faysal's second reign, 1843-1865, was destined to become the high point of the Saud's leadership in the nineteenth century. In the words of Bayly Winder, Imam Faysal was:

> Farsighted enough to realize that he could not convert the whole world to Wahhabism, and that if he tried he would again bring ruin on his people and himself. . . He was a devout Wahhabi, but, instead of attacking Karbala, he received a British diplomat (Col. Lewis Pelly) in his capital [Winder, 1965: 228].

More importantly, he restored order to the Najd and reasserted Saudi authority north to the Jabal Shammar and south to Oman. Saudi control of the Buraymi Oasis during Faysal's reign became the basis of the subsequent Saudi claim to the oasis against the claims of Abu Dhabi and Oman, not settled until 1974 with the Saudis withdrawing their claim for other territorial concessions.

Faysal's death marked yet another of the seemingly periodical eclipses of Saudi power. Two of his sons, Abdallah, who succeeded him, and Saud, were bitter rivals and engaged in civil war between 1865 and 1889. Saud ousted his brother in 1871 and ruled until his death in 1875 when Abdallah again became Imam. By this time, however, Saudi rule was fatally weakened. The Eastern Province (Hasa) was lost to the Ottomans in 1871, the Jabal Shammar revolted, and in 1887 the Saudi state again collapsed. Central Arabia came under the control of Muhammad

Ibn Rashid, Amir of the Shammar, who ruled from the Jabal Shammar capital at al-Hayil.

A third son of Faysal, Abd al-Rahman, served briefly as Rashidi governor of his family's former capital, Riyadh, but after an abortive uprising in 1891, he fled with his family to Kuwait.

From the humiliating exile in Kuwait arose the modern state of Saudi Arabia. It was the accomplishment of one man, Abd ál-Aziz bin Abd al-Rahman bin Faysal Al Saud, known throughout the world as Ibn Saud. Abd al-Aziz was a striking figure; well over six feet tall and handsome, he was the kind of man who commanded attention. In the desert tradition he had many wives and children and was a master of tribal politics and warfare.

What really set Abd al-Aziz apart from his contemporaries, however, was his breadth of vision. During his long career, he looked beyond the parochial interests of his people and dealt on equal terms with Western diplomats, soldiers, businessmen, and oil-men. Although he did not fully foresee it at the time, these dealings were to transform Saudi Arabia totally from an inward-looking desert principality to a major world economic power.

The story of how Abd al-Aziz retook Riyadh is now legendary. During the winter of 1901-1902, Abd al-Aziz and a group of followers left Kuwait, travelling south and east. Nearing Riyadh, he selected a force of 40 men and on the night of January 16, 1902, they stole over the city wall. Concealing themselves near the al-Mismak fortress where the Rashidi governor, Ajlan, spent the night as a security precaution, they waited praying and planning for the dawn when he would leave the fort.

When the morning came and Ajlan and some of his retinue stepped out of the fort, they were immediately set upon by Abd al-Aziz and his followers. Leaving Ajlan, his men ran back through the fortress gate. Abd al-Aziz's cousin, Abdallah bin Jaluwi, threw a spear at Ajlan which missed and broke off in the gate where it is imbedded to this day.

The struggle was brief. Ajlan ran for the gate, and for a brief moment his men and Abd al-Aziz played tug-of-war with his body. He was finally pulled through, but before the gate could be closed, Abd al-Aziz's men, led by Abdallah bin Jaluwi, broke through, slew the governor and all resistance ended. Abd al-Aziz had won back his capital. It now remained for him to win back his country.

Restoring the Saudi patrimony took Abd al-Aziz nearly 20 years. Although the Rashidi Amir, Abd al-Aziz Ibn Rashid, was killed by Saudi troops in 1906, it was not until 1922 that he finally subdued the Ibn Rashids and captured their capital, Hayil. In the meantime, he recaptured eastern Arabia from the Turks, subdued the Bedouin tribes, and created a powerful military force, the Ikhwan (the Brethren) from Bedouins converted to Wahhabism.

During this period, World War I focused the attention of the European powers on Arabia. Of the three principal rulers in Arabia, Saud Ibn Rashid sided with the Turks and Germans whereas Abd al-Aziz and Sharif Husayn of the Hijaz sided with the British. The war also brought two famous Britons to the peninsula. Col. T. E. Lawrence (Lawrence of Arabia) encouraged Sharif Husayn to revolt against the Ottoman Sultan and lead Arab assaults against Turkish troops along the Hijaz railway in raids which have since become legendary. In 1917, the British sent a mission to Abd al-Aziz to persuade him to cooperate with the allies and Sharif Husayn and to attack the Ibn Rashids. One member of the mission, Sir John B. Philby, stayed on in Arabia to become a renowned author, explorer, and confidant of Abd al-Aziz.

With the war over, Abd al-Aziz finally crushed the Ibn Rashids, and Sharif Husayn proclaimed himself "King of the Arabs." Despite British urging, relations between Husayn and Abd al-Aziz had never been good. In 1912, Husayn seized Abd al-Aziz's brother Sa'd and released him only after imposing humiliating terms on Abd al-Aziz. In 1919, Abd al-Aziz's son, later King Faysal, visited London. Traveling on to Paris when the Versailles Peace Conference was under way, he met Husayn's own son Faysal, who snubbed him.

One cause of Najdi-Hijazi friction was control of the Utaybah tribal region adjacent to the Hijaz but Najdi in outlook. Husayn sent a force under his son Abdallah to capture the Utaybah town of Kurmah. Camped nearby at Turabah, the army was virtually wiped out by Abd al-Aziz's Ikhwan. An Utaybah tribesman who was at the battle told the writer that only those with horses (about 100 including Abdallah) escaped. "Thank God I had a horse," he added, indicating for the first time which side he was on.

Though nothing lay between the Sauds and Mecca, Abd al-Aziz did not press his advantage. In 1924, at the dissolution of the Ottoman Caliphate, Husayn declared himself Caliph of all Muslims. This was more than Abd al-Aziz could accept and he invaded the Hijaz. Taif was taken without resistance, but when an unexplained shot was fired, the zealous Ikhwan sacked the city. Terrified Hijazis, when they heard the news, pressured Husayn to abdicate in favor of his son Ali. But Ali fared little better than his father and in January 1926 he, too, departed from Jiddah into exile.

In a quarter of a century Abd al-Aziz, starting with 40 men, had expanded his control to include nearly all the kingdom's present territories. (In 1934 after a brief war with the Yemen led by his son Faysal, Abd al-Aziz consolidated Saudi control of Asir, a process which had begun in 1924, thereby establishing Saudi control of the Wadi Najran.) He had adopted the title Amir of Najd after his capture of Riyadh and, later, Sultan of Najd. After the capture of Hijaz, he adopted the title King of Najd and the Hijaz. Finally, in 1932, he consolidated the two into the Kingdom of Saudi Arabia.

The history of Saudi Arabia since 1932 has been one of breathtaking economic and social change. The enabling factor was oil, discovered in 1938. By the time Abd al-Aziz died in 1953, his government was firmly committed to the development of his people.

He was succeeded by his eldest surviving son, Saud. A product of an earlier time, Saud was not able to cope with the modernization made possible by growing oil wealth. His reign was characterized by palace intrigue and heavy spending, and even with its vast oil income, the Saudi treasury was almost empty at times. In 1964, the royal family and religious leaders, acting in accordance with Islamic law, chose his brother Faysal to succeed him. Saud left the country and died in Athens on February 23, 1969.

King Faysal reigned from 1964 to March 25, 1975, when he was shot by a nephew over what is generally considered to have been a family grievance. At the time of his death, Faysal had been in public life longer than any contemporary head of state. Beginning with his official visit to London when he was barely 14 years old, Faysal's public career covered a span of 56 years. In terms of the social change and development of his country from an insignificant desert amirate to a world oil power, his experience spanned centuries. As a boy and a young man, he grew up with the age-old and turbulent political traditions of the desert. In later years, he became an international figure and elder statesman, chosen, for example, as *Time* magazine's "Man of the Year" for 1974 (*Time,* 1975: 8-32).

He was made Viceroy of the Hijaz soon after it was conquered by his father in 1926. Under his brother King Saud, Faysal presided over the Council of Ministers until differences of views brought his retirement in the early 1960s. During that period, he was responsible for restoring the financial health of the kingdom. By the time he ascended the throne in 1964, he had already had considerable experience in statecraft.

Faysal continued the economic and social development policies started in his father's reign. While still crown prince and prime minister in 1962, he introduced his ten-point program of social and economic reform which was to be the guideline for development until the first five year plan in 1970. The Reform Program also embodied the late king's desire to preserve the traditional Islamic social order based on the strict teachings of the Wahhabi revival. To the extent that his social and economic goals came into conflict with each other, Faysal moved slowly, never wanting to get too far ahead of his people.

It was in the field of foreign affairs that King Faysal's true interests and greatest talents lay. He was appointed Foreign Minister in 1930, a post he held but for one brief period for the rest of his life. In 1945 he attended the San Francisco Conference, and during his career he travelled to Middle Eastern and Western capitals and to the United States.

Faysal's foreign policy was based on preserving the Islamic world and its way of life. As keeper of the two most sacred sites in Islam, Mecca and al-Madinah, Faysal felt that Saudi Arabia must play a special role in protecting Islamic values from the onslaught of the atheistic doctrines of socialism and communism. In seeking to curb this threat, he looked to the West and particularly to the United States for political and military support. For Faysal, the other major threat to the Islamic world was Israel. Not only did Israel occupy Arab soil, but since 1967 it had occupied the third most holy site in orthodox or Sunni Islam, the Aqsa Mosque in Jerusalem.[7] It had been Faysal's desire to pray in that mosque before he died. The fact that Faysal's chief protector against communism, the United States, was also the chief supporter of Zionism made Faysal's foreign policy somewhat ambivalent and often widely misunderstood. To the extent that his policy against the communist-zionist threat appears inconsistent in the West, however, Faysal was equally convinced that U.S. support of Zionism, which he blamed for the spread of radicalism in the Arab world, was highly inconsistent with U.S. policy opposing communism. Towards the end of his life, he tried to convince the United States of what he thought was the error of its ways. It was in this context that he determined to use oil as a weapon in 1973. Hearing of the U.S. intention to supply Israel with $2.2 billion in military and other aid during the October 1973 Arab-Israeli war, he initiated the Arab oil embargo.

Faysal was succeeded by his half-brother Khalid and another brother, Fahd, was appointed crown prince. Many had thought that Faysal would outlive his brother, since Khalid had had two massive coronaries and open-heart surgery in 1969. Yet he appears to have recovered from his operation and is in tolerably good health. Because he was a retiring man who had taken little interest in politics, it was also widely thought that the crown prince would take a major role in day-to-day decision-making. King Khalid, however, has shown a keener interest in politics than many had supposed. Thus far, his policies have followed in the footsteps of his brother and father before him, emphasizing economic development and social reform.

III. POLITICS AND THE POLITICAL PROCESS

The activities of the royal family and those of the national government are quite distinct in Saudi Arabia, even though the same individuals are often involved in both. Politically the royal family serves as the country's constituency. The king must maintain its support to stay in power. This constraint, plus those imposed by Islamic law which serves as the constitution and legal system of the country, means that a Saudi king is not the absolute monarch described by outside observers.

The Saudi Royal Family

Relatively little is known about the manner in which the royal family gives or withdraws its support. Formally it is done through a venerable Islamic institution known as *ahl al-aqd wal-hall* (The People Who Bind and Loose). This institution consists of the royal family and leading religious and government leaders, but the preponderant power within it is the royal family. It was convened in 1964 when support was withdrawn from King Saud in favor of his brother, King Faysal. The decision was given Islamic legal sanction by a *fatwa,* or Islamic legal opinion. Presumably this institution also functioned, though perhaps not formally, in installing King Khalid as the successor to King Faysal in 1975, and Prince Fahd as crown prince.

The functioning of the *ahl al-aqd wal-hall* is a manifestation of the royal family political process rather than a description of it. Members of the royal family tend not to discuss the workings of the family and much of what is known about it is based on deduction from those few instances when its activities come into public view.

Basically, it works, as do many institutions in the Arab world from families to governments, on the traditional concept of *ijma'* (consensus). Throughout Saudi history, when royal family consensus was strongly behind a ruler, the monarchy flourished. When there was no consensus, as has occurred several times in the past, the monarchy fell on hard times or was even temporarily superseded. One of the present day concerns of the royal family is that the consensus of support for the ruler should not be undermined, for the survival of the monarchy could be at stake.

In attempting to deduce how the royal family creates or maintains a consensus, a great deal can be learned from its organizational structure. First of all, the degree of influence a single member might have depends in great part on his generation. Since the death of King Abd al-Aziz, kingship has passed from brother to brother among his sons. Yet, at this writing, at least three of the brothers of Abd al-Aziz are still living—Prince Abdallah, Prince Ahmad, and Prince Mus'ad—and on royal family matters, their voices carry the weight of an older generation.

Among the sons of King Abd al-Aziz, including the present king, mutuality of interests often converges around full brothers. Abd al-Aziz had during his lifetime many wives (though in accordance with Islamic law no more than four at one time). Many of these marriages were made for political and tribal reasons. His many children, therefore, are half brothers except in cases where they have the same mother, and sons of the same mother tend to stick together.

The king has one full brother, Prince Muhammad. Older than Khalid, Muhammad is the senior surviving brother. Disqualified from ascending the throne for reasons of personal health, Muhammad renounced his claim to be crown prince in 1964 in favor of his younger full brother Khalid. Similarly, when Prince Fahd was chosen crown prince in 1975, two half brothers, senior to him, Nasir and Sa'd, also renounced their claims.

One of the largest and best known of these sibling groups is the Al Fahd, or Family of Fahd, so named after the eldest, Crown Prince Fahd. Seven brothers in all, they are also called the "Sudayri Seven" after the maiden name of their mother, Hussah bint al-Sudayri. Six of the seven brothers are prominent in government. There are also several other groups among the surviving brothers. Although full brothers tend to gravitate toward one another, it would be a mistake to assume that all royal family politics revolve around sibling loyalties. These groupings constantly split and reconstitute themselves on specific issues.

In addition to the sons and brothers of King Abd al-Aziz, there are three collateral branches of the royal family that play an important role in consensus-making. One, the Saud al-Kabir branch, descends from Amir Saud (al Kabir), twelfth ruler of Najd (1869-1875) and an elder brother of King Abd al-Aziz's father, Abd al-Rahman. Since this branch is therefore senior to the present line, its head, Muhammad Saud al-Kabir, ranks in royal family protocol second only behind the king.

A second collateral branch, the bin Jaluwis, descend from Jaluwi, a brother of King Abd al-Aziz's grandfather. Jaluwi's son, Abdallah bin Jaluwi, was one of the original 40 men who recaptured Riyadh with King Abd al-Aziz in 1902. He was subsequently appointed Amir of the Eastern Province, was succeeded by his son, Saud, and at his death, by a second son, Abd al-Muhsin who still retains the position. The mother of King Khalid and Prince Muhammad, Jawhara bint Musa'd, was also a bin Jaluwi as is Haya bint Turki, mother of King Faysal's two sons, Khalid and Sa'd.

The third collateral branch, the Thunayans, descend from Thunayan, an older brother of the founder of the Saudi dynasty, Muhammad bin Saud. This branch produced one Saudi ruler, Abdallah al-Thunayan (r. 1841-1843), and later descendents moved to Ottoman Turkey. Ahmad al-Thunayan, who was reared in Turkey, returned to Najd where he became a close confidant of

King Abd al-Aziz. It was he who accompanied the then Prince Faysal to London and France in 1919. Ahmad died in 1921. Eleven years later, Faysal visited his widow in Istanbul while returning from a visit to Europe and Russia, and invited her and her daughter to visit Riyadh. Soon after their arrival, he married the daughter, Iffat, who became a favorite and wielded a strong influence on the future king.

A number of other Thunayans followed her from Turkey and the branch's influence in royal family affairs has risen greatly.

Toward the end of Faysal's reign, Iffat became known in Saudi Arabia as "the queen." This was a mark of special respect since, in the Saudi system, the wife of a king has never been considered a queen. In addition to her interest in public affairs, Queen Iffat also became active in business. She owns a modern office building and apartment complex in Jiddah. Known as the "Queen's building," it dominates the skyline.

The grandsons of King Abd al-Aziz constitute another group within the royal family. Of a younger generation, their views do not as yet carry the weight in royal family circles that those of their elders do, but many of them do have the added advantage of a formal education. For example, with the exception of his eldest son Abdallah, King Faysal required all of his sons to receive a university education in the United States or Britain. Other grandsons have also attended U.S. and British universities. Collectively they represent a new class of "royal technocrats." It is with this group that the future of the monarchy rests.

National Policy-making

Policy-making within the national government in Saudi Arabia can be characterized as the fusion of a traditional, highly personalized decision-making process practiced by King Abd al-Aziz and his predecessors with a burgeoning bureaucratic structure. Before the capture of the Hijaz, Abd al-Aziz governed Najd in a patriarchal style that was well suited to the conservative Arabian heartland of that day. When he conquered the Hijaz, however, he inherited a much more sophisticated system of government, complete with cabinet ministers. Originally Najd and the Hijaz were ruled as two separate countries, united only in the person of the ruler. In 1926, an Organic Law for the Kingdom of the Hijaz was promulgated entrusting its administration to the then Prince Faysal as viceroy. In 1931, the Hijazi government was further streamlined and emerged with a cabinet comprised of Ministries of Finance, Interior, and Foreign Affairs, and a Consultative Council. Under the Ministry of Interior were Departments of Public Health, Public Instruction, Posts and Telegraphs, Maritime Health and Quarantine, Public Security, Islamic Courts and Municipalities. Najd, in the meantime, was still governed for the most part in the same traditional manner of personal consensus.

This division of the two governmental systems, however, did not always work out that way in practice. For if the king wished the Hijazi bureaucracy to perform a service in Najd, it was done. Faysal's viceregal decrees, moreover, were often also applied in Najd, whereas in the Eastern Province, Abdallah bin Jiluwi was given wide discretionary powers and administered his territories with an iron hand. In short, personalities counted far more than formal governmental institutions.

In 1930, Faysal was appointed overall foreign minister, and in 1932 the Hijaz and Najd were formally joined in the Kingdom of Saudi Arabia. Gradually, the Hijazi administrative structure began to disappear and many of its functions were absorbed by the national Ministry of Finance, headed for years by the legendary Abdallah Sulayman. In 1954 it was merged with the Ministry of National Economy to form the Ministry of Finance and National Economy.

Gradually other ministries appeared, many originating as departments under the Finance Ministry. One of King Abd al-Aziz's last acts before his death in 1953 was to create a Council of Ministers. By 1970, the number of Ministries had risen to 14, and in 1975 it increased to the present 20.

Among the new ministries created in 1975, the Ministry of Planning illustrates the rapid development of Saudi governmental structure. Originally created as the Central Planning Organization in the early 1960s, it was largely moribund for a number of years. The whole concept of central planning required more cooperation among the ministries than they, jealously guarding their prerogatives, were prepared to give. In 1968, however, the CPO got a dynamic young director, Hisham Nazir, and under his directorship two five year plans were developed, and the CPO was ultimately raised to ministry status.

Local government structure in Saudi Arabia has developed along lines similar to national government, but has not attained the same degree of sophistication. Moreover, with bureaucratic decision-making becoming increasingly centralized, the power of the provincial amir is considerably weaker than in the days when the Hijaz and the Eastern Province were administered almost as separate fiefdoms under the king.

There has recently been discussion about entirely revamping the local government structure. At the time of this writing, however, the country is still divided into 18 provincial amirates. Five—Mecca (including Jiddah and Taif), Riyadh, the Eastern Province, the Northern Frontiers, and Hayil—are called major amirates and their amirs all report directly to the Minister of the Interior. Qasim and al-Madinah are administered as major amirates and their amirs also report directly to the minister, but they are considered somewhat less important. The others report to the deputy minister.

The most onerous task confronting the Saudi bureaucracy is the annual Hajj or Pilgrimage to Mecca. It occurs each year during the Muslim lunar month of Dhu al-Hijjah, which means that its solar calendar date falls 11 days earlier each year.

When one considers that roughly 1,500,000 Hajjis (pilgrims) arrive each year from all over the Muslim world as well as from all parts of Saudi Arabia, speaking scores of languages, predominantly elderly, and all requiring food, shelter, sanitation, and transportation under harsh physical conditions including a scorching desert climate, one can begin to see the magnitude of the problem facing the Saudi government.

Basically, each Hajji must perform a number of required rites, many of which predate Islam, for Mecca was a religious center long before the birth of Muhammad. It was Muhammad, however, who took these rites and fashioned them into the Islamic pilgrimage, one of the five pillars of Islam.

The rites include the *Tawwaf,* or seven-fold circumambulation of the Ka'bah, the rectangular stone structure in the center of the great Haram Mosque; the *Sa'y,* or seven-fold trek between al-Safa and al-Marwah, two elevated points near the Haram Mosque; the recitation of sunset prayers on the plain of Arafat near Mecca on Standing Day *(Yawm al-Wuquf),* the ninth day of Dhu al-Hijjah; sacrificing a blemishless animal during the *'Id al-Adha* (Feast of the Sacrifice), a festival held throughout the Muslim world on the 10th, 11th, and 12th of Dhu al-Hijjah; and throwing ritual stones at the three *jamras* (pillars representing shaytans "satans") in Mina, a small town near Mecca. A visit to al-Madinah, while not required, is generally undertaken by most Hajjis. Most of the rites can be done at different times, but the Standing Day and Feast of the Sacrifice are done by all at the same time and the same place. The logistics of transportation alone during these periods are staggering.

Both the physical as well as the spiritual needs of the Hajjis are met by a group of private individuals who have performed these services for centuries. They are organized into highly specialized guilds: the *Mutawwifs,* who serve in effect as religious tour directors, organizing the journeys of the Hajjis and looking after them during their stay in Mecca; the *Zamzamis,* who provide daily water from the holy Zamzam well and perform other tasks; the *Dalils,* who look after the Hajjis in al-Madinah; and the *Wakils,* who serve as agents and deputies to the Mutawwifs and are mainly located in Jiddah, the principal air and sea terminus for Mecca.

Until the Saudis conquered the Hijaz in 1924-1926, these guilds systematically exploited the Hajjis. The Saudis, however, have endeavored to insure the welfare of the Hajjis by imposing strict regulations on the guilds. For example, today the guilds must charge a fixed fee for their services which is collected not by them but by the government as added protection to the Hajji.

Even though the needs of the Hajjis are thus actually met by a heavily regulated but nevertheless private sector service industry, there is scarcely a ministry or government agency that does not in some fashion get involved in the Hajj. Much of the administrative responsibility is under the jurisdiction of the Ministry of Hajj and

Aqaf (singular *waqf,* an Islamic religious endowment). Overall governmental administrative coordination, however, is directed by the Higher Hajj Committee, chaired by the Amir of Mecca; its members include municipal leaders of Jiddah and Mecca and regional representatives of various ministries. The committee begins work each year several months before the Hajj to formulate plans for Hajj administration.

Among the other ministries with major responsibilities during the Hajj are Interior, which provides security and traffic control; Foreign Affairs, which must issue special Hajj visas and perform protocol functions for VIP Hajjis; and Defense and Aviation, which, *inter alia* is in charge of air traffic. Jiddah Airport during the Hajj is the busiest in the world. The Health Ministry must supervise sanitation and quarantine. The latter, subject to international supervision until 1957, is particularly sensitive because of the prevalence of infectious diseases such as cholera in many Muslim countries.

On balance, the Hajj is administered rather well considering the still evolving stage of development of the Saudi bureaucracy and the monumental tasks involved. Since the trend has been toward even larger numbers, however, the burden of administering the Hajj is likely to become even greater.

The military structure of Saudi Arabia has undergone a metamorphosis similar to the civilian bureaucratic system. Following the capture of the Hijaz in 1926, King Abd al-Aziz's tribally-based and fiercely religious Ikhwan warriors grew restless and in 1929 a group of them mutinied. In what was probably the last great Bedouin battle, Abd al-Aziz defeated them at Sibila. One of their leaders, Faysal Darwish of the Mutayr tribe, was captured, pardoned, struggled for a lost cause briefly, and then went into exile to Iraq. Other leaders were subsequently imprisoned or went into exile. The days of the Bedouin as a political-military power were over and by World War II Saudi Arabia had virtually disbanded its armed forces.

In 1944, a new Ministry of Defense (later Defense and Aviation) was created. Three years later, in 1947, the United States established a military air field at Dhahran which included facilities for training a modern Saudi air force. A British mission arrived the same year to train a modern army. It was replaced by a U.S. Military Training Mission (USMTM) in 1952 with advisory functions in all branches of the armed forces.

The U.S. training mission did not, however, result in a modern armed force overnight. For one thing, the Saudi leadership, well aware of the potential threat of a modern armed force to the monarchy, did not really wish the Americans to be too successful in their training role. One of the major justifications for USMTM in Saudi eyes was that it provided a physical earnest of U.S. support for the regime against communist or other radically inspired military threats. As an additional precaution, a tribally based, paramilitary force, the National Guard, was created parallel to the army to serve as the monarchy's primary internal security force.

In the 1960s, events forced the Saudis to rethink their security needs. In 1962, the monarchial regime in the Yemen was overthrown by Egyptian-backed republicans. Ultimately, a 60,000 man Egyptian military force entered the Yemen to maintain the republican regime, and was considered a definite threat to the Saudis who backed opposition royalist forces. The Egyptian-Yemeni threat did not abate until 1967 when the Egyptian forces were pulled out on the eve of the June War. Subsequently, good relations were restored between Saudi Arabia and both the Yemen and Egypt. King Faysal, having ascended the throne in 1964, was nevertheless convinced that Saudi Arabia must have a credible military force and turned to the United States for assistance. His views were reinforced by the Arab defeat in 1967. Saudi troops did not participate in the 1967 war, but Faysal was convinced that Saudi Arabia would be inevitably drawn into any succeeding Arab-Israeli war, and that its troops must give a good account of themselves. Late in the same year, a radical regime came into power with independence in South Yemen. Its militant radicalism, in the Saudis' view, threatened the stability of the entire Arabian Peninsula. The South Yemenis lost no time in supporting the Dhufar rebels in neighboring Oman, straining relations with North Yemen and actually precipitating a brief military clash with Saudi Arabia in late 1969. (By 1976, however, the Dhufar rebellion was quelled and Saudi Arabia and South Yemen had moved closer to a policy of peaceful coexistence.)

In early 1968, the British announced their intention of withdrawing from the Gulf, focusing regional and international attention on Gulf security. Later in the year, an Iranian gunboat seized an ARAMCO off-shore oil drilling rig in what was a larger territorial dispute over the location of a Gulf median line dividing Saudi and Iranian off-shore drilling rights. The dispute was resolved but this, plus the imminent British departure, added to Faysal's determination to develop a naval capability both in the Gulf and the Red Sea. At the same time, the Saudis concluded that the National Guard also needed to be up-graded to keep pace with the armed forces. Accordingly, a modernization program was established which is still in effect.

The most visible arms acquisitions have been made by the air force. By the mid-1960s, Saudi pilots were still flying obsolescent F-86s, and the Royal Saudi Air Force (RSAF) sought to up-grade its inventory with American F-104s. The United States, however, partly to aid the ailing British aircraft industry, encouraged the Saudis to buy British Lightnings as part of a larger air defense system which also included U.S. Hawk surface-to-air missiles. The total sales package amounted to several hundred million dollars. At the same time, the RSAF bought a number of Lockheed C-130 transport aircraft.

The Saudis never found the Lightnings satisfactory. Requiring a relatively high degree of maintenance, they were seldom over 50 percent operational at any given time. In the early 1970s, the Saudis began to purchase U.S. manufactured F-5s. These were not intended as a replacement for the Lightnings, but had the latter been more reliable the Saudis probably would not have proceeded so rapidly—that is, had they purchased F-104s in the first place, the Saudis probably would have been satisfied with fewer F-5s and not given the impression to outside observers of a "massive arms build-up." Unfortunately, this impression might be strengthened in the near future as the Saudis seek a follow-on aircraft for the aging Lightnings. Yet it was known a decade ago that the Lightnings would become obsolescent about this time.

The Saudi army also underwent an expansion and development program including a major effort to upgrade its mobility. Additionally, Saudi troops were assigned to Jordan to train with the Jordanian Arab Army. These troops were sent to the front during the 1973 Arab-Israeli war.

Naval expansion, beginning with only a few hundred officers and men, has proceeded more slowly. The Saudis, however, are developing a major naval installation at Jubayl, on the Persian Gulf, and one on the Red Sea as well.

These expansion programs have all contributed to upgrading the armed forces, now numbering around 42,000, and the National Guard, numbering around 33,000. Moreover, the Ministry of Interior has also initiated programs to improve the capability of the National Police and the Coast Guard and Frontier Force. Despite much progress, however, the Saudi military and security establishments cannot be considered as strong as those of the Arab states confronting Israel. In a purely military context, the latter face a much more immediate threat which demands a high degree of preparedness. Having fought several wars with Israel, they also have more combat experience. In addition, the manpower constraints generally affecting Saudi Arabia also affect its armed forces. For example, as soon as a soldier receives training as an automobile mechanic, it becomes a great temptation for him to leave the service and enter the private sector where he can command much higher wages. As a result, the Saudis must spend additional sums on inducements to keep up the morale of their military and security forces.

The major arms build-up in Saudi Arabia over the last 10 years, therefore, is the result of several factors: the perception of a radical threat first from the Yemen and then from South Yemen and probably also Iraq; Saudi Arabia's greater role in Arab-Israeli dispute; the momentum of follow-on arms purchases to up-grade original purchases made a decade ago; and the feeling of inadequacy in military preparedness as the British left the Gulf all contributed. When compared with Iran's military build up, Western critics often conclude that Saudi Arabia is engaging in an arms race with the Shah. The Saudis, however, do not see their desire to strengthen their military posture as aimed against the Shah, but rather that they must have a credible armed force if they are to be equal partners with the Shah in Persian Gulf security. Arms race or not, however, the arms transfers to the Gulf area in recent years have been impressive, and the Saudi military establishment has expanded considerably.

The Saudi legal system has also undergone evolution, albeit strictly within the framework of the Shari'a or Islamic law. In Islamic legal theory, the law is God's word. All activities are relegated to five categories: those which are mandatory, recommended, forbidden, discouraged, and finally those about which there is no mention in the holy law. The sources of the law are the Our'an and the Sunna (sayings or "traditions" of the Prophet, Muhammed). Because the law is divinely inspired, no man can make laws in the Western sense. The Hijaz did have a *Majlis al-Shura,* or Consultative Assembly, which had a quasi-legislative function; and there is now discussion of instituting a nation-wide assembly. Theoretically, however, it would not draft laws but regulations *(nizams)* pertaining to those areas not covered in the holy law. At present, nizams are decreed by the king.

The ruler *(Imam)* is the chief administrator of justice in Islamic law. Thus, while he is the final court of appeal, the law exists independently of his will and he could actually be sued in his own court. The ruler delegates his authority to judges *(qadis).* In theory, a plaintiff needs no lawyer, for his case will be judged by divine law. In practice, he may have a lawyer or "agent."

The origin of the present legal system in Saudi Arabia dates back to 1926 when King Abd al-Aziz issued an order unifying the judicial system under the Hanbali School of Islamic Law and abolishing customary tribal law. In 1965, there were over 200 courts in the land and in 1970 the number was 3,500 and growing. By that year, moreover, the Shari'a law colleges of al-Madinah and Riyadh and the Islamic School of Education in Mecca were integrated into Riyadh and Abd al-Aziz Universities in order to provide more qualified judges, lawyers, and court clerks.

In 1970, King Faysal initiated a great step toward modernization, establishing a Ministry of Justice to administer the legal and judicial system. By integrating it more closely within the governmental structure, he enabled it to be more responsive to rapidly changing Saudi society.

Social change, however, had already prompted other changes. The legal questions arising from dealings with oil companies and other foreign corporations and governments necessitated the establishment of procedures and institutions outside the Islamic legal system. Nearly every ministry now retains Western trained lawyers (called "legal advisors" as distinct from *muhamis* or Shari'a lawyers). A Commercial Court also exists under the Ministry of Commerce to adjudicate commercial disputes. Created in 1926 originally only for the Hijaz, it was abolished in 1955 but recreated in 1962. Under the new Labor Law of 1969, a system of Labor Disputes Arbitration Committees was also created to hear labor disputes.

A more fascinating administrative tribunal, however, is the *Diwan al-Mazalim,* or Board of Grievances. Based on pre-Islamic Persian legal tradition and adapted to Shari'a law, it was historically used to complement the *Quda* (regular Islamic) courts in extraordinary cases of injustice, and was based on the right of the ruler to adjudicate all injustices. In Saudi Arabia, a Grievance Board was established in 1955, as an administrative tribunal primarily for cases involving complaints against governmental administration. Its jurisdiction also includes bribery cases and cases involving the Arab boycott of Israel. The creation of the Saudi Board of Grievances thus demonstrates that despite the very conservative nature of Hanbali Islamic law, the Saudis have been able to fashion traditional institutions to meet their present needs.

The monumental changes in public administration in Saudi Arabia in the past half-century have had an almost incalculable influence on governmental decision-making. The creation of institutions and standardized procedures has removed much of the ad hoc quality that marked the government of King Abd al-Aziz. It would be a mistake, however, to assume that the creation of a government bureaucracy has appreciably depersonalized the Saudi system of government. Rather, personal relationships, which are still the key to Saudi decision-making, have been circumscribed by an institutional framework through which decisions must now be channeled.

For example, prior to the creation of the Supreme Petroleum Council in 1973, all of those appointed to it were already the key advisors to the king on oil matters. However, when two of the members subsequently died, the institutionalization of the policy process required that two new members be appointed. Had there been no council, no replacements would have been necessary.

There are three loci of decision-making powers in the Saudi government. Most routine decisions are made at the ministry level and each ministry carefully guards against inroads into what it perceives to be its rightful area of responsibilities. For example, the Ministries of Education and Higher Education share responsibility for the Saudi school system. But the University of Petroleum and Minerals is administered by the Ministry of Petroleum and Mineral Resources, and the Saudi vocational school system is administered by the Ministry of Labor and Social Affairs.

Moreover, within each ministry, there is often very little delegation of authority so that decisions tend to be made by the minister and his principal lieutenants.

Major decisions affecting the country at large are made by the other two loci, the royal family and the senior technocrats. Virtually all of the major positions affecting national security are held by members of the royal family. The king is president of the Council of Ministers; Crown Prince Fahd is First Deputy Premier and head of the Supreme Petroleum Council, and Prince Abdallah is Second Deputy Prime Minister and head of the National Guard. The Minister of Defense, Prince Sultan, and the Minister of Interior, Prince Nayif, as well as the vice ministers of Defense and Interior, are full brothers of Prince Fahd, members of the "Sudayri Seven." The foreign minister, Prince Saudi bin Faysal is the son of the late king and thus represents a junior sibling group within the family.

There are two other members of the royal family who were appointed to the Cabinet in 1975—Prince Majid bin Abd al-Aziz, Minister of Municiple and Rural Affairs, and Prince Mit'ab bin Abd al-Aziz, Minister of Public Works and Housing. These two portfolios are not national security oriented, however, and a number of observers feel that the appointment of these younger half-brothers of the king was made in an effort to balance the royal family appointments which tend to gravitate toward the "Sudayri Seven" on the one hand and Prince Abdallah (who has no full brothers) on the other. Another result of the cabinet change of 1975 was the addition of two additional members of the Al al-Shaykh. The appointment of the new Minister of Justice, Shaykh Ibrahim Al al-Shaykh, restores to the family the highest Islamic juridical position in the land. A second member of the family, Dr. Abd al-Rahman Al al-Shaykh, Minister of Agriculture and Water, also has the distinction of being a technocrat. In his early 30s, he received a Ph.D. in the United States. The Minister of Higher Education, Shaykh Hasan Al al-Shaykh, was also in the previous Cabinet.

Royal family members also govern the major provinces. Nearly all the rest are in the hands of the Sudayri family which is closely related to the Al Sauds by marriage.

There was some speculation that the 1975 Cabinet, which added six new portfolios for a total of 20, would see even more members of the royal family appointed. Such was not the case. In ministries requiring technical expertise, the Saudis have shown themselves determined to appoint qualified people. Among the better known technocrats are Muhammad Aba al-Khayl, Minister of Finance and National Economy; Ahmad Zaki Yamani, Minister of Petroleum and Mineral Resources; Ghazi al-Qusaybi, Minister of Industry and Electricity; Hisham Nazir, Minister of Planning; and Abd al-Aziz al-Qurayshi, Governor of the Saudi Arabian Monetary Authority (the central bank).

Virtually every major Saudi government decision involves some configuration of these royal family members and technocrats and generally proceeds from consensus. It is easy to see that with such responsibilities falling on such a few shoulders, important decisions can often become delayed simply because of the limitations of time. With the great expansion of bureaucratic responsibility inherent in the ambitious new Five Year Plan, a serious bottleneck in getting decisions made is increasing. As work piles up, however, decisions are being forced on more junior people. In the long run, therefore, the concentration of decision-making among such a relatively few people could presage a more efficiently operating bureaucracy.

IV. THE SAUDI ECONOMY

Looking at the oil-based affluence of Saudi Arabia today, it is difficult to recall that not very many years ago the Saudis were on the verge of poverty. Throughout the nineteenth and first quarter of the twentieth centuries, the Saudi regime led a meager existence. Its revenue requirements were modest, being predominantly needed for financing wars or preventing them. But expenditures often exceeded revenues, and Saudi rulers constantly sought outside subsidies, generally from the Ottomans or the British.

After conquering the Hijaz in the mid-1920s, the Saudis' chief source of public revenue became the Hajj. Ironically, Saudi efforts to prevent economic exploitation of the Hajjis thus worked against the country's own economic interests. Far more disastrous from an economic point of view, however, was the great decline in numbers of those making the Hajj in the 1930s. There were two major reasons for the decline. First, the Great Depression made it financially more difficult, and second, the deteriorating international situation before World War II made it politically more difficult to make the trip. Thus, while King Abd al-Aziz was able to reduce the financial exploitation and other abuses formerly experienced by Hajjis, decreasing Hajj receipts forced him to raise Hajj fees, thus perpetuating the commercialization of the Hajj by the public as well as the private sector. So precarious were the finances of Saudi Arabia during this period that the Minister of Finance, Abdallah Sulayman, was able to keep the entire financial records of the kingdom in a large ledger which he purportedly kept under his bed at night.

The Making of An Oil Kingdom

All this changed abruptly after World War II when Saudi oil began to flow in commercial quantities. The first Saudi oil concession was awarded to an entrepreneur from New Zealand, Major Frank Holms. The concession, which he sold to Standard Oil of California (Socal) was later allowed to lapse. In 1933, Socal–with the aid of the British explorer, writer and confidant of King Abd al-Aziz, H. St. John B. Philby, and an American who had studied Saudi geology, Karl Twitchell–obtained a new concession. A wholly owned subsidiary, the California Arabian Standard Oil Company (Casoc) was created to prospect for oil.

Saudi oil was discovered in 1935, but it was in 1938 when "Dammam No. 7" was spudded in that the company first knew it had oil in commercial quantities. World War II temporarily halted the development of Saudi oil production, however, and so only after the war did the country begin to reap the benefits of its oil resources.

In 1936 Socal, which had surplus oil, and Texaco, which had extensive markets, joined forces overseas. Their joint company, Caltex, took charge of Saudi operations. On January 31, 1944, Casoc's name was changed to the Arabian-American Oil Company (ARAMCO). Four years later Jersey Standard (EXXON) and Standard of New York (Mobil) also bought into ARAMCO, making it a totally owned subsidiary of four major American oil companies.

Even with vastly increased revenues from oil in the immediate postwar period, the state of Saudi finances was not always secure. Even oil revenues could not always keep up with the heavy spending of the 1950s. Toward the end of the decade, a Pakistani monetary expert, Anwar Ali, was brought in on loan from the International Monetary Fund to stabilize Saudi currency as head of the central bank, the Saudi Arabian Monetary Agency (SAMA). Since then, Saudi fiscal and monetary policies have been conducted with great conservatism and responsibility, making the Saudi Riyal (SR) one of the most stable currencies in the world even before the monumental rises in foreign reserves in the 1970s.

Throughout the 1960s, rising world demand for oil was rapidly approaching production capacity. Because of huge proved reserves and two generations of oil glut, the impending shift from a buyers' to a sellers' market and resulting price rises were not immediately foreseen in either the consuming or the producing countries. The end of the decade saw a number of events which hastened the process. The 1967 Arab-Israeli war closed the Suez Canal and put an added strain on supply at a time when some countries such as Libya were cutting production as a part of a conservation policy. More importantly, the United States, which had always been the world's largest producer, was expected to reach a peak in production by 1970.

Between 1970 and 1973, the oil producing countries gained control over pricing from the companies. In addition, the oil producing countries were well on their way to gaining outright control of the oil producing facilities as well. As early as 1967, the Saudi Petroleum Minister, Shaykh Ahmad Zaki Yamani, first announced a plan whereby the producing states would eventually buy out the oil companies' producing operations. Called "participation," the scheme was initially met with skepticism. But in December 1972 an agreement for 25 percent "participation" or equity was reached in several Gulf countries including Saudi Arabia, and in June 1974 ARAMCO agreed to 60 percent Saudi participation. In March 1976 Saudi Arabia entered into negotiations for control of ARAMCO's remaining equity, years ahead of what even Yamani had projected.

In October and December of 1973, the price doubled and doubled again. Since the first price rise came during the October 1973 Arab-Israeli war which also resulted in the Arab embargo, the two have been closely associated in the minds of many Westerners. In fact, the two were quite different in nature. The

October price rise was the result of a collective decision of the Organization of Petroleum Exporting Countries (OPEC), including non-Middle East producers, and was dictated almost entirely by economic considerations.

The embargo, on the other hand, which actually came in effect after the first price rise, was initiated only by the Arab oil producers under the auspices of the Organization of Arab Petroleum Exporting Countries (OAPEC), and was instituted for political reasons. During the previous year, King Faysal had publicly and privately warned Western oil men, newsmen and politicians that if the West, particularly the United States, did not adopt what he perceived to be a more even-handed policy regarding the Arab-Israeli conflict, the Arabs would have no choice but to use the oil weapon. So angry was he when he heard of the $2.2 billion U.S. military aid to Israel announced during the war, that he resolved to impose the embargo. Because of Saudi Arabia's commanding position in oil production, King Faysal was able virtually single-handedly to make the embargo work, even though it was conducted under the auspices of OAPEC. With world production near its peak, there was no other country which had the excess capacity to compensate for the production restrictions imposed by the Saudis and other Arab producers.

The embargo did have an influence on the second price rise in December. By creating an even shorter supply situation, it enabled OPEC producers led by Iran again to raise the price. Ironically, King Faysal was not in favor of the second price hike. It was not that he opposed rising oil prices but rather that he felt that two precipitous price rises in rapid succession could create serious dislocations in the free world economy. This, he believed, might not only economically weaken the free world, of which all the oil producers were a part, but might also weaken the West's ability to combat the spread of communism. For Faysal, these factors together with Zionism, comprised the principal political threats to Saudi Arabia and the Muslim world generally.

Faysal revoked the embargo in early 1974. That summer, Yamani let it be known that Saudi Arabia would have an oil auction, which a number of observers thought would lower the price of oil. The auction never materialized and the Saudis were accused variously of bad faith and weakness in not standing up to Iran and other OPEC members that wished prices to stay up. A more plausible explanation would be that Faysal, a strong man but a man of agreement, preferred not to flout OPEC opinion.

Whatever incremental adjustments may occur in the future price of oil, the Saudis will continue to dominate world production for the foreseeable future. With proved oil reserves conservatively estimated at around 152 billion barrels, the largest in the world, and a relatively low absorptive capacity for capital investment compared to its massive revenues, Saudi Arabia has the discretionary capability to set price and production rates for at least the medium term. There are, however, several factors which would constrain Saudi Arabia from using this capability arbitrarily. One is its preference for working within OPEC's consensus rather than in the face of it. The Saudis are determined not to undermine OPEC's role in setting price and production levels.

A second factor is that economic realities have forced the other producers closer to the Saudi position. The world recession of 1974-1975, combined with higher oil prices, reduced demand considerably. Initially such producers as Iran needed high prices at fairly high production rates to finance ambitious economic development plans; therefore, they relied on countries with a lower absorptive capacity for capital expenditure to take the brunt of production cuts needed to keep prices up. Thus, while Saudi Arabia's production capacity has been raised to over 12 million barrels per day, it was in early 1976 producing at only about two-thirds' capacity. Some observers, therefore, predicating their conclusions on the view that Saudi Arabia would not accept disproportionate production cuts indefinitely, predicted the imminent demise of OPEC. Such predictions were premature, however. For one thing, they underestimated the psychological glue binding the OPEC members together on oil matters. Equally important, the depressed market finally forced other countries, including Iran, to cut production despite revenue needs, and the real price of oil has also moderated. This has been accomplished by price freezes and more modest price rises allowing world inflation to lower real prices, and by proliferation of special discounts by various producing countries.

World demand for oil is expected to rise in the latter half of the decade with recovery from the current recession. Depending on political as well as economic factors and policies of the major producing and consuming states not now precisely known, upward pressure could again be put on oil prices. In any event, Saudi Arabia can be expected to continue as a moderating force among the OPEC members.

The Structure of the Saudi Economy

By 1973, over 90 percent of the Saudi gross national product was oil related, and after the four-fold price rises, the percentage has increased. For all that, however, few Saudis are actually employed in this capital-intensive industry. Most Saudis are still employed in agriculture and nomadic herding. The farms are mostly small holdings in the great oases of the Eastern Province, the smaller but more numerous oases of Najd, and the irrigated and dry farming areas in the Hijaz Mountains and Asir.

Despite a large agricultural labor force, less than one percent of the land is arable, and the Saudis have to import most of their food. Consequently, agriculture has received much government attention and expenditure.

Based on a major water resources study in the 1960s, a program was developed for drilling wells and "mining" water. In addition, a number of large scale agricultural projects were begun. One of the most ambitious was a major land reclamation project at the great Hasa Oasis. Centuries of primitive irrigation had made large areas of the oasis too saline for cultivation, and an extensive plan for draining and leaching the soil was drawn up. Begun in 1966, the project was completed in 1972 with an expenditure of SR 260 million ($57.7 million according to the 1971 exchange rate). It is expected to support an increased agricultural population in Hasa of some 50,000 persons on some 12,000 hectares of reclaimed land.

Also in 1971, the Wadi Jizan dam was completed, being the first stage in a larger project to capture run-off water from the mountains and use it for irrigated agriculture on the Tihamah plain below. With a capacity of 71 million cubic meters of water, the dam was built at a cost of SR 42 million ($9.3 million). Another dam, at Abha, completed in 1974, cost SR 29 million ($8.4 million according to the 1974 exchange rate), and has a capacity of 2.4 million cubic meters of water.

An agricultural scheme with a social as well as an economic goal in mind is the Bedouin settlement and land reclamation project at Haradh. The King Faysal Model Settlement Scheme, as it is called, was completed in 1972 at a cost of SR 100 million. While it has been successfully operating since that time, however, its initial expectations have not been entirely realized. In many cases, the proud and independent Bedouin have preferred their traditional way of life and shunned the economically more lucrative but also more confined way of life of sedentary farmers.

In addition to these projects, agricultural extension services have been expanded, well drilling has continued, an agricultural school has been opened at Buraydah, and farm subsidies are being introduced.

Although the Saudi industrial sector has been dominated by the oil industry, there has been in recent years an attempt to diversify. The principal organization for industrial development is Petromin (the Petroleum and Minerals Organization), founded in 1962. Projects begun by Petromin include the steel rolling mill at Jiddah, which started production in 1968, the Jiddah oil refinery for domestic production which came on stream in 1968, and the Saudi Arabian Fertilizer Company (SAFCO) which began production in 1969.

Outside the agricultural sector and the government bureaucracy, most Saudis are employed in service industries, with Hajj-related services being one of the most extensive. Because the Hajj is seasonal, however, with many part-time workers and many enterprises only partially devoted to the Hajj trade, it is difficult accurately to estimate the size of the private sector Hajj service industry by numbers or occupation. For example, despite huge public and private expenditures, the Hajj still generates the single greatest source of retail commercial activity in the kingdom, somewhat akin to the Christmas season in the United States. In earlier years, Hajjis came primarily by land and sea, and stayed longer periods of time, sometimes a year before returning home. In the jet age, the Hajj season has been shortened to roughly six weeks. Still, for many Jiddah, Mecca, and al-Madinah merchants one-third of their sales are made during that period. Hajj charter flights have also been one of the major reasons why Saudi Airlines has grown into one of the Middle East's largest carriers since it was founded in 1949.

Commercial activity when added to annual public expenditure on the Hajj probably generates over a half-billion dollars in income, mainly in the Hijaz. While small in terms of GNP, the commercial aspects of the Hajj are nevertheless a major means of income generation and distribution.

Economic Development, Foreign Aid, and Foreign Investment

Prior to 1968, government-financed economic development projects were largely uncoordinated and often overlapped. Without a basic infrastructure and because of the time required for changing public attitudes through education and other social welfare projects, the pace of development probably could not have been accelerated. The foundations for educational, health, communications, and other programs were laid, and although performance on particular projects was occasionally uneven, overall economic and social development was impressive.

In 1970, the Central Planning Organization, after two years work, launched the country's first five-year plan. The main goal was diversification of Saudi Arabia's single commodity (oil) economy, and the plan called for investment in agricultural development and industrialization. Initially SR 41.3 billion was allocated to the plan, but after the oil price hikes of 1973, it was expanded by 35 percent.

The Saudi economy grew very rapidly during the period of the first five-year plan. In constant prices, the gross domestic product (GDP) increased from a 13.1 percent growth rate in 1970 to a compound rate of 20.5 percent in 1973. In addition to the agricultural and industrial projects, economic and social infrastructure projects were also begun and expanded.

From 1970 to 1975 the number of hospitals rose from 47 to 62, an increase of 569 beds. More significantly the quality of health care was greatly improved. At the same time the national road network increased to nearly 7,000 miles of paved roads and is still expanding. Communications were also expanded, but not fast enough to keep pace with even greater demand. The same was true of housing.

In 1975, Saudi Arabia announced its second five-year plan with a budgeted expenditure of $149 billion. It proposes to continue along the same lines as the first plan, with emphasis on agriculture, industrialization, particularly in petrochemicals, and economic and social infrastructure. The magnitude of the plan is a reflection of the great increase in Saudi financial resources. Bottlenecks already appearing during the period of the first plan will probably place even greater strains on the current plan.

The greatest bottleneck is the lack of manpower at all levels of the economy. With a population base of less than four million Saudis out of a total of between five and six million residents, Saudi Arabia simply does not have the manpower to accomplish all the development projects which its financial resources enable it to afford without extensive imports of foreign labor and expertise.

The manpower problem, however, is more complex than a shortage in numbers. It is also in part a problem of social attitudes. Many Saudis, particularly those of a nomadic tribal origin, find manual labor and even some skilled professions to be demeaning. For example, such jobs as plumbers, painters, and construction workers are almost impossible to fill with Saudis. Ironically, the same stigma does not apply to electricians and chauffeurs whose work is associated with science and technology. Largely as a result of these attitudes, most of the manual labor in Saudi Arabia is performed by foreigners, notably Yemenis. It is estimated that over one million Yemenis are currently employed in Saudi Arabia, predominantly as unskilled and semi-skilled workers. Many other nationalities are also represented in the labor force. They include Palestinians, Jordanians, Syrians, and

Egyptians, who are employed mainly as white collar workers, clerks, and school teachers; Pakistanis, including a large number of physicians as well as clerks and white collar workers; and, of course, Western technicians, particularly Americans.

Another social constraint on manpower resources is the role of women. In the West, for example, a much greater proportion of women would be at work than is the case in Saudi Arabia. This attitude is slowly changing, partly through education and increasing contacts with the outside world but also as a result of the increasing demand for labor. Restricted domestic manpower resources have forced the Saudis to import large numbers of foreign laborers and technicians. According to the Minister of Industry and Electricity, Dr. Ghazi al-Qusaybi, Saudi Arabia intends to import half a million workers to meet the requirements of the second five-year plan. If dependents are added to the total, it will raise the number of foreigners in the country even more. The bulk of the workers are expected to come from the Yemen, Egypt, Turkey, Pakistan, India, South Korea, and Taiwan, and managerial and technological experts from Western Europe and the United States.

The implications of such a large scale importation of manpower are immense. Sociologically, the impact of diverse peoples and cultures suddenly placed in close proximity with a conservative and heretofore relatively isolated Saudi population is impossible to gauge, except to say that the pace of social change, already rapid, will become even more so. There may well be political repercussions. Kuwait already presents itself as a model of a country with an alien majority which does not participate in the political process. In Saudi Arabia the scale would simply be larger. This is not to say that such a situation is necessarily politically destablizing, or that the foreign laborers, providing their economic and material expectations are met, would even desire participation in the political process. But a large foreign work force is bound to add a new dimension to Saudi domestic politics, no matter what form it might take.

There is an additional complication arising from the manpower shortage. Since the 1973 oil price rises, all of the oil producing countries in the Gulf region have greatly expanded their development programs. Countries such as Kuwait and the UAE already have to depend on predominantly foreign labor forces. But even Iran, with a population of 33 million, expects to create half a million jobs for which there are no qualified Iranians. Thus, the Saudis will be competing with all of these countries for the same types of manpower, a situation which will make the shortages of labor in the Middle East even more acute.

Another bottleneck caused by increasing orders for the Saudis' expanded development programs has clogged the seaports of the country. There was by the spring of 1976 an incredible 120 day turn-around time for ships in Jiddah port.

A shortage of berths and unloading facilities is only a part of the problem; with skyrocketing real estate costs, many importers still find it cheaper to leave materials in the port and pay port charges rather than clear them for storage elsewhere. In other cases, earlier bottlenecks have slowed projects down so that by the time later shipments do arrive, they cannot yet be used. From the air the congestion at Jiddah port, with so many ships riding at anchor, resembles nothing so much as the Normandy invasion.

Whether or not these and other bottlenecks affect the pace of Saudi Arabia's ambitious development plans, the country will still probably earn more from oil than it will be able to spend over the near term. Foreign aid could absorb some of the petrodollars. Indeed, Saudi Arabia is working to develop a more comprehensive and integrated approach to foreign aid.

In earlier years, foreign aid was generally given on an ad hoc basis, or channeled through such institutions as the Muslim World League. With the large increase in revenues after 1973, however, the Saudis have expanded their foreign aid programs, both in magnitude and in institutional machinery.

Among the decisions taken has been to increase Saudi participation in the International Monetary Fund as a part of a multilateral approach to foreign aid. For bilateral and regional projects, a number of institutions have been created, the most important being the Saudi Arabian Development Fund. The major targets of Saudi aid are the non-oil producing Arab states such as Egypt and the Sudan, the rest of the Muslim world, and finally the rest of the Third World in general. To facilitate development financing in these countries, several institutions have been or are being established. They include the Arab Bank for Economic Development in Africa, the Arab Fund for Economic and Social Development, the Islamic Development Bank, and the Saudi-Egyptian Company for Industrial Investments.

Despite this impressive array of institutions, however, development programs outside Saudi Arabia are likely to face many of the bottlenecks experienced within Saudi Arabia—lack of skilled manpower (particularly where local labor is drawn to the oil producing states by higher wages) and a lack of economic and social infrastructure. Because of these limits on the absorptive capacity of capital in most of the Third World, it is unlikely that foreign aid expenditures, whether grants or concessionary financing, will meet the expectations or at least hopes of many of the potential recipients.

The greatest proportion of Saudi Arabia's immense revenues—its foreign exchange holdings are now second only to West Germany's—must be invested in the major money markets of Western Europe and the United States, therefore, at least in the near term. During the Arab oil embargo period there was much anxiety, almost verging on hysteria in some cases, that the Saudis and other Arab oil states might use their massive reserves to achieve political ends. This anxiety was reinforced by the Saudi preference for short term deposits, despite lower returns and, in some cases, even negative interest rates.

Saudi investment policy, however, quite contrary to such fears, was probably overly conservative and was certainly not politicized. The Saudis was fully aware of their own growing stake in a stable world monetary system. Their investment policy simply reflected a preference for security and liquidity over risk and return on investment. The priority given to security was probably influenced, at least in part, by fears of Western intentions. Thus, while there were those in the West who feared punitive transfers of Arab reserve deposits or politically inspired investment to control certain Western companies or banks, the Saudis saw pressures in the West to limit or control their investments as a sign that such investments would be insecure for political reasons.

Since 1974, much of the initial anxiety on both sides has receded. The Saudis, realizing that even the major banks could not absorb such massive deposits in short term notes, have begun to make longer term investments in the Western money markets and to diversify their investments as well. Thus, the "crisis" of recycling petrodollars, if it ever existed, is to a great extent over. Barring another major political crisis such as renewed Arab-Israeli hostilities, the mutual trust between the Saudis and other oil producer investors on the one hand, and the Western money markets on the other, is likely to continue to improve.

The Saudi Private Sector

Saudi Arabia has one of the most laissez faire economies in the world. The Hanbali School of Islamic Law, while very conservative in its religious and social aspects, is actually one of the most liberal on business affairs. For example, although Saudi Arabia refuses to engage in political or diplomatic relations with communist states, there is no prohibition against buying products from these countries. Goods from China and Eastern Europe are found in the *suqs* (markets) of all the Saudi towns and cities.

There is also a different business ethic in Saudi Arabia than in many non-Islamic countries. Stealing is not tolerated; the traditional Islamic punishment is to cut off a hand of one so convicted. As a result, except in urban areas where "Western" attitudes are being introduced, one's personal property is still inviolate. Moreover, under the traditional system, a man's word is his bond, and since business relations are still highly personalized, one almost never hears of a Saudi businessman going back on his word once given, regardless of the legal arrangements.

At the same time, the overriding business principle is "buyer beware." Failure by a Western businessman to understand this could lead to disastrous results. Another major principle, widely misunderstood in the West, is that it is not necessarily morally reprehensible to accept a payment for a service rendered, even in cases which to a Westerner would verge on bribery or graft. Moreover, although no payment is expected if no service is rendered, there is no restriction against asking for one. In effect, it is up to the other party to decide whether a request should be met. Moreover, this principle has tended to weaken the concept of conflict of interest as it is known in the West. Saudi political figures, therefore, are commonly investors in Saudi commercial enterprises, often in partnership with old established business families or younger, Western-educated Saudi entrepreneurs.

To anyone who has ever lived in the Middle East, this ethic is easily recognizable and widely prevalent. The difference in Saudi Arabia and other oil producing states, however, is the magnitude of the transactions, often in the millions of dollars.

Despite the free market philosophy in Saudi Arabia, the overwhelming position of oil has caused the public sector to dominate the economy, as it does in all the Middle Eastern oil producing states. The government, therefore, has reluctantly found itself playing the leading role in the economy.

The old merchant families were traditionally distributors of goods and services and, except for construction and real estate, have been reluctant to invest their own capital in domestic ventures. This has changed somewhat with government encouragement. For example, private capital has recently been invested in a joint venture with General Motors to build a truck assembly plant. Still, private capital plays a relatively small part in economic development. The private sector role has primarily been one of either bidding directly on government-financed development projects or brokering as agents for foreign companies competing for tenders.

In some cases, foreign private capital is also encouraged on a joint venture basis, always with controlling interest in Saudi hands. Obviously, capital financing is not the primary consideration in joint ventures. Generally, underlying such a venture is the desire to acquire technology, a ready-made market outlet, or simply to assure the outside company's continuing interest in the venture because of its equity position.

In sum, the Saudi economy has made tremendous strides since the first commercial-scale oil production began shortly after World War II. Because of its huge oil revenues, however, Saudi Arabia's financial ability to initiate development programs far outstrips its manpower resources and the economic and social infrastructure necessary to sustain such projects at peak efficiency. These problems are being met in part by importing needed manpower and by expanding infrastructure projects, but bottlenecks still exist. Thus, despite expansion of foreign aid programs, most Saudi revenues must, at least for the near term, still be invested in the money markets of the West.

The Saudi economy is basically laissez-faire, but is dominated by the public sector due to its immense oil revenues. The government has therefore in effect become the senior partner in a system of "Islamic state capitalism."

V. PROBLEMS AND PROSPECTS

The interaction of the old and the new runs throughout Saudi politics, economics, and society and is at once the country's greatest strength and greatest potential weakness. The ability of the Saudi regime to adapt to change has stood the test of over 200 years. The pace of change in the country today, however, far outstrips anything that even the most visionary observer could have predicted just a few short years ago. One can literally see it in the skylines of Jiddah and Riyadh as new buildings rise apparently every month or so. The challenge to the Saudi leadership, therefore, has never been greater.

Saudi Arabia's place in contemporary world affairs is derived from sales of its huge oil reserves and the resultant accumulation of foreign exchange far beyond the absorption capacity of its present economy. Since this *petropower,* as some have called it, is almost entirely economic in nature, the area in which Saudi policies will make the greatest impact is in international economic relations. To be sure, the Saudis can and have used their oil for political ends, as shown by the Arab oil embargo of 1973-1974. Even then, however, it was the prevailing market. conditions which enabled the embargo to become effective—conditions which did not prevail during the abortive oil embargo following the June 1967 Arab-Israeli war.

There are a number of major constraints against Saudi Arabia using its *petropower* arbitrarily for either political or economic ends. Politically, the Saudis view a strong free world economy as essential to preventing the spread of communist and other radical ideologies which they view as inimical to their Muslim way of life. Any policies which would tend seriously to undermine the free world economy would therefore not be deemed in their best interest. The Saudis realize that with their rapidly expanding foreign reserve holdings they have a growing stake in the health of the free world economy. Whatever hurts the economy of the free world will hurt them also.

The Saudi government shows every intention of continuing to work through OPEC. Those who predicted the demise of OPEC a year or so ago greatly underestimated the determination of Saudi Arabia and other OPEC members to stand together on price and production rates. At the same time, there are definite differences in the economic interests of the two leading OPEC consensus makers, Saudi Arabia and Iran. The latter prefers high production rates and high prices to maximize oil revenues commensurate with its ambitious development plans. The Saudis do not consider that they need the income generated by high production rates and feel that prices are sufficiently high for the present in view of the urgency of having the world economy recover more fully from the recent recession.

This difference in perceived economic interests was reflected in the OPEC conference in Bali in May 1976. At that meeting, the Saudi view prevailed and prices were not raised as the Iranians and others wished them to be. Market factors, also, greatly contributed to keeping prices stable. For, although world oil demand was again rising by mid-1976, it had not fully recovered from the recession and was still not sufficiently strong to precipitate a major price hike.

In the future, the Saudis can be expected to continue to exert a moderating influence on OPEC oil prices. They cannot be expected, however, to hold prices down unilaterally for an indefinite period even though they have the capability to do so. One can assume that their own national interests as perceived will govern their actions in regard to oil production rates and prices.

Market forces, moreover, will continue to play a strong role in determining how strongly the Saudis hold the line.

Saudi foreign investment policies will probably continue to reflect a growing sophistication in terms of overall Saudi economic interests. Investment priorities are turning increasingly toward longer term investments, less liquidity, and greater diversification. The trend is based in great measure on greater mutual trust by Saudi investors and Western money markets. However, if, as a result of a major crisis such as the renewal of Arab-Israeli hostilities either side resorted to punitive economic or financial measures, the progress toward greater cooperation could quickly erode. Such a situation would have a disastrous effect on the international monetary system. The Saudis are already the second largest foreign reserve holder behind West Germany and could well be first in a few years.

Turning to Saudi-U.S. relations, Saudi policy will probably continue to be somewhat ambivalent. The principal Saudi foreign policy goal is to preserve Islamic values in Saudi Arabia and the Muslim world in general. They seek to accomplish this with the cooperation of the Western powers against the mutual threat of communism and radicalism. The great dilemma facing the Saudis, however, is that the United States, which the Saudis see as the principal protector against communism, is also seen as the principal protector of Zionism. Thus, in the context of confronting communism, Saudi relations with the United States will continue to be very friendly. In the context of U.S. support for Israel, however, the Saudis will continue to try to convince their friends the Americans to be more "even-handed." Moreover, if the Arab-Israeli problem erupts into fighting again, the crisis could sour Saudi-U.S. relations on a much broader front.

Despite political differences over Zionism, the Saudis have had long and quite warm economic and technological ties with the United States. ARAMCO's relations with the Saudi government, for example, have been excellent and remain so even after Saudi plans have been set in motion to take control of ARAMCO's remaining equity in oil production. ARAMCO is expected to remain in Saudi Arabia as a service company and continue to play an important role in Saudi oil production. If it had not been for

ARAMCO's past record and the mutual trust built up over the years, this would probably have not been the case.

The Saudi affinity for U.S. business practices and technology gives a decided comparative advantage to U.S. firms seeking to participate in the country's ambitious development plans. This advantage, however, is tempered by the relative disadvantage U.S. firms face in competing with European and Japanese firms which can get concessionary financing from their home governments. Some overtures have been made to the Saudis to change their bidding requirements, in order to make them more competitive, but little headway has been made. By the same token, the U.S. government has been traditionally disinclined to subsidize U.S. exports. Thus it is doubtful whether U.S. firms will be able to overcome their disadvantage in financing in the near future. This will continue to have the greatest effect on smaller firms since their ability to obtain financing and performance bonds for multimillion dollar projects is more limited.

The chances for the success of Saudi foreign policy are in some measure dependent on external forces. Despite its growing stature in Arab politics, for example, Saudi Arabia is not a major confrontation state against Israel. Political decisions in Cairo, Damascus, Amman, and Tel Aviv, therefore, in addition to those in Washington and Moscow, will continue to be major determinants of Saudi policy options on Middle East peace, including the option of a renewed Arab embargo. Saudi Arabia's oil and economic policy options, by the same token, are also highly dependent on external economic forces and OPEC solidarity.

With so much outside interest on Saudi Arabia's role in world affairs, it is sometimes overlooked that the major determinants of Saudi policy-making are internal and domestic in nature. In the long run, the viability of the regime will depend on its ability to cope with the rapidly rising expectations of its people. The chief aim of Saudi domestic policy has been to provide material advancement while preserving the traditional Islamic religious and social structure. Yet implicit in material welfare is educational advancement, a breeding ground for new ideas challenging the old. The very success of Saudi development programs, therefore, has created an escalation of expectations. But the Saudi regime has not provided institutionally for broad public participation in the political process. Traditionally, participation was gained largely through interpersonal relationships, exemplified by the late King Faysal's insistence on conducting a weekly public *Majlis* where his people could address him. But today, the pressures of running a modern state have virtually precluded systematic personalized communication between ruler and ruled. Recognizing this, the government is considering ways to increase public participation in the political process. One idea is to create a Consultative Assembly. Yet, in the long run, it is probably not so much what the government does as whether its actions keep ahead of public expectations that will determine the future stability of the regime.

In fact, political aspirations have been overshadowed by economic aspirations, and as long as economic expectations are satisfied, pressure for increased political participation could continue to be relatively light. The vast increase in wealth since 1973, however, has added new strains. For example, the magnitude of some government projects has enabled successful businessmen to reap huge fortunes, producing a more visible gap between the rich and the poor. Inflation, including sky-rocketing real estate prices, has also exacerbated the problem of income distribution by making it more difficult for those of medium income levels to maintain a constant standard of living. Land in the major cities is so expensive that it is now sold by the square meter, and Western-style houses rent from $25,000 to $50,000 per year.

The ability of the traditional Saudi system of business ethics to cope efficiently with multimillion dollar transactions has also come under scrutiny. Without assuming moral superiority for Western business ethics, one may question whether traditional Saudi business methods are up to the task of implementing the country's ambitious development plans, and whether or not a more disciplined system of accountability might be required.

All of these problems are multidimensional, yet none is insoluble. Most significantly, Saudi leaders are aware of them and are attempting to find solutions. On balance, the chances for success seem fairly bright, given sound leadership and political foresight. Saudi Arabia's efforts to use its vast oil wealth to develop a modern society with age-old Islamic values makes it one of the most exciting places to watch in the Middle East.

NOTES

1. The exact size is indeterminable since most of its southern borders are as yet undemarcated.

2. The Muslim era begins in 622 A.D., the year of Muhammad's flight from Mecca to al-Madinah. The flight, called the Hijrah, begins the Muslim or Hijriyyah calendar. A lunar calendar of 12 months, it is 11 days shorter than the solar calendar. Hijriyyah dates are rendered A.H. The year 1395 falls in 1975-1976 A.D.

3. Ibn and bin both mean "son of" and can be used to connote an actual father or a family's founder.

4. The term amir like the term shaykh has many meanings in Arabic. As the head of an amirate or shaykhdom, they mean ruler. In Saudi Arabia, amir is now used to refer to a provincial governor or a royal prince. Shaykh is an honorific term referring to an elder, a statesman, or a religious figure. Abd al-Wahhab was known as *the* Shaykh, in this case meaning religious teacher. After the revival took hold, Saudi rulers became known as imams. An imam is a leader of the faithful or umma. As such, umma has the meaning of nation with a heavily Islamic connotation.

5. The Hanbali School is the most conservative of four Sunni schools. The others are Hanafi, Malki, and Shafi'i. Each is named for its founder.

6. The term Wahhabi was originally used by opponents of the revival. Wahhabis usually prefer to be called Muwahidin, or "unitarians," a term that refers to their strict monotheism.

7. This is not the famous gold-domed Mosque of Omer or Dome of the Rock, but a less imposing silver-domed mosque near by.

SELECTED BIBLIOGRAPHY

ABIR, M. (1974) Oil, Power and Politics: Conflict in Arabia, The Red Sea and the Gulf. London: Frank Cass.

ADELMAN, M.A. (1972-1973) "Is the oil shortage real? Oil companies as OPEC tax collectors." Foreign Policy, 9 (winter): 69-107.

AKINS, J.E. (1973) "The oil crisis: This time the wolf is hers." Foreign Policy, 51, 3, (April): 462-490.

ARAMCO Handbook. (1968) Dhahran: Arabian American Oil Co.

BENOIST-MECHIN, J. (1955) Ibn Seoud: ou le Naissance d'un Royaume. Paris: Editions Albin Michel.

BURRELL, R.M. and A.J. COTTRELL (1972) Iran, The Arabian Peninsula and the Indian Ocean. Strategy Papers, 14. New York: National Strategy Info. Center.

BURTON, R.F. (1898) Personal Narrative of a Pilgrimage to al-Madinah and Meccah. 2 vols. London: George Bell & Sons.

COOPER, C.A. and S.S. ALEXANDER [eds.] (1972) Economic Development and Population Growth in the Middle East. New York: American Elsevier.

DE GAURY, G. (1966) Faisal: King of Saudi Arabia. London: Arthur Barker.

DOUGHTY, C.M. (1888) Travels in Arabia Deserta. Cambridge: Cambridge Univ. Press.

DUGUET, F. (1932) Le Pelerinage de la Mecque au Point de Vue Religieux, Sociale et Sanitaire. Paris: Editions Reider.

HOLDEN, D. (1966) Farewell to Arabia. London: Faber & Faber.

HOWARTH, D. (1964) The Desert King: Ibn Saud and His Arabia. New York: McGraw-Hill.

KNAUERHASE, R. (1975) The Saudi Arabian Economy. New York: Praeger.

LAWRENCE, T.E. (1935) Seven Pillars of Wisdom. Garden City: Doubleday.

LONG, D.E. (1976 forthcoming) The Hajj Today: A Survey of the Contemporary Mecca Pilgrimage. Washington: Georgetown Univ. Center for Contemporary Arab Studies and the Middle East Institute; New York: State Univ. Press.

--- (1976) The Persian Gulf: An Introduction to Its People, Politics and Economics. Boulder, Colorado: Westview.

MEULEN, D. Van Der (1957) The Wells of Ibn Sa'ud. New York: Praeger.

NAKHLEH, E.A. (1975) The United States and Saudi Arabia: A Policy Analysis. Washington: American Enterprise Institute for Public Policy Research.

NALLINO, C.A. (1939) L'Arabia Saudiana. Vol. 1 of Raccolta de Scritti Editi e Inediti. M. Nallins (ed.) Rome: Istituto per l'oriente.

NEIBUHR, C. (1972) Travels Through Arabia. 2 vols. Edinburgh: G. Mudie.

PHILBY, H. St. John B. (1955) Saudi Arabia. London: Ernest Benn.

——— (1953) Arabian Jubilee. New York: John Day.

——— (1930) Arabia. London: Ernest Benn.

——— (1928) Arabia of the Wahhabis. London: Constable.

RATHJENS, C. (1948) Die Pilgerfarht nach Mekka Von der Weihrauchstrasse zur Olwirtschaft. Hamburgh: Robert Molich Verlag.

RIHANI, A. (1928) Ibn Sa'oud of Arabia. London: Constable.

SEARBY, D.M. (1976) "Doing business in the Mideast: The game is rigged." Harvard Business Rev., 54, 1 (January-February): 55-64.

STOCKING, G.W. (1970) Middle East Oil: A Study in Political and Economic Controversy. Nashville: Vanderbilt Univ. Press.

THESIGER, W. (1959) Arabian Sands. New York: Dutton.

Time (1975) January 6: 8-32.

U.S. Department of Treasury, U.S.-Saudi Arabian Joint Commission on Economic Cooperation. (1975) Summary of Saudi Arabian Five Year Development Plan (1975-1980). Washington: U.S. Gov. Print. Office.

WAHBA, H. (1965) Arabian Days. London: Arthur Baker.

WINDER, R.B. (1965) Saudi Arabia in the Nineteenth Century. New York: St. Martins Press; London: MacMillan.

TABLE 1
BASIC INFORMATION

OFFICIAL NAME:	The Kingdom of Saudi Arabia
CHIEF OF STATE:	King Khalid bin Abd al-Aziz Al Saud
AREA:	Approximately 830,000 square miles
POPULATION:	Approximately five million (including resident aliens)
CAPITAL:	Riyadh
MAJOR CITIES:	Jiddah, Riyadh, Mecca, al-Taif, al-Madinah, Damam, al-Khúbar, Abha Jizan
UNIT OF CURRENCY:	Saudi Riyal (SR) SR 1 = $ .29
OIL PRODUCTION (1975):	7.1 million bpd
OIL INCOME (1975):	$27.1 billion
TOTAL IMPORTS (1975)	$5.7 billion
PROVED OIL RESERVES (1975):	151.8 billion barrels

TABLE 2

ABBREVIATED GENEOLOGY OF THE AL SAUD

(Numbers and dates indicate rulers and the period of their reign)

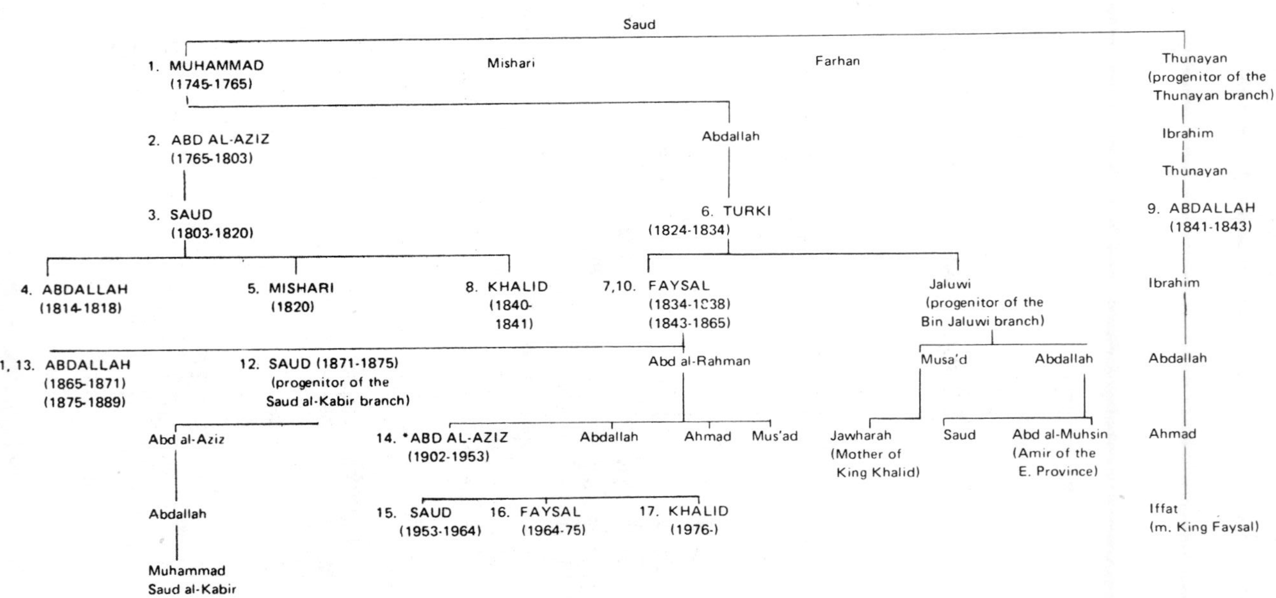

TABLE 3
THE FAMILY OF KING ABD AL-AZIZ*
(Mothers' names in parentheses)

ABD AL-AZIZ
(r. 1902-1953)

Turki (d. 1919)	(Wadhba bint Hazzam)	(Tarfah bint al-Shaykh)	(Jawharah bint Musa'd Bin Jaluwi)	(Bazza)	(Jawharah bint Sa'd al Sudayri)	(Hussah bint al Sudayri)	(bint Asi al-Shuraym)
	SAUD (r. 1953-1964, d. 1969)	FAYSAL (r. 1964-1975)	Muhammad b. 1910	Nasir b. 1920	Sa'd b. 1920	Fahd b. 1920	Abdallah b. 1923
			KHALID b. 1912 r. 1975-	Bandar b. 1923	Musa'id b. 1923	Sultan b. 1924	
				Fawwaz b. 1934	Abd al-Muhsin b. 1925	Abd al-Rahman b. 1926	
						Nayif b. 1933	
						Turki b. 1934	
						Salman b. 1936	
						Ahmad b. 1937	

Sons of FAYSAL:

(Sultana bint Ahmad al-Sudayri)	(Haya bint Turki Bin Jaluwi)	(iffat al-Thunayan)
Abdallah b. 1923	Khalid b. 1941	Muhammad b. 1937
	Sa'd b. 1942	Saud b. 1941
		Abd al-Rahman b. 1942

TABLE 3 (Continued)

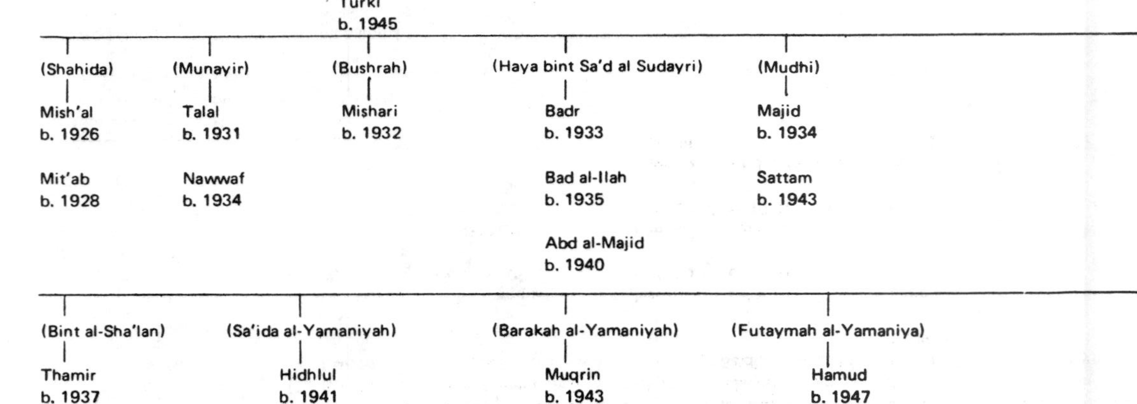

*With the exception of the first three, the chart includes only surviving sons.

TABLE 4
PRINCIPAL GOVERNMENT OFFICIALS

KING AND PRIME MINISTER	Khalid bin Abd al-Aziz Al Saud
FIRST DEPUTY PRIME MINISTER & CROWN PRINCE	Fahd bin Abd al-Aziz Al Saud
SECOND DEPUTY PRIME MINISTER	Abdallah bin Abd al-Aziz Al Saud
MIN. OF AGRICULTURE & WATER	Dr. Abd al-Rahman bin Abd al-Aziz Al al-Shaykh
MIN. OF COMMERCE	Dr. Sulaiman Abd al-Aziz al-Sulaim
MIN. OF COMMUNICATIONS	Muhammad Umar Tawfiq
MIN. OF DEFENSE & AVIATION	Sultan bin Abd al-Aziz Al Saud
MIN. OF EDUCATION	Dr. Abd Al Aziz Abdallah al-Khuwaiter
MIN. OF FINANCE & NATL. ECONOMY	Muhammad Aba al-Khail
MIN. OF FOREIGN AFFAIRS	Saud ibn Faisal bin Abd al-Aziz Al Saud
MIN. OF HEALTH	Dr. Hussain Abd al-Qadir al-Jazairi
MIN. OF HIGHER EDUCATION	Hasan bin Abdallah Al al-Shaykh
MIN. OF INDUSTRY & ELECTRICITY	Dr. Ghazi Abd al-Rahman al-Qusaybi
MIN. OF INFORMATION	Dr. Muhammad Abdu Yamani
MIN. OF INTERIOR	Nayif ibn Abd al-Aziz Al Saud
MIN. OF JUSTICE	Ibrahim bin Muhammad bin Ibrahim Al al-Shaykh
MIN. OF LABOR & SOCIAL AFFAIRS	Ibrahim bin Abdallah al-Anqari
MIN. OF MUNICIPAL & RURAL AFFAIRS	Majid bin Abd al-Aziz Al Saud

MIN. OF PETROLEUM & MINERAL RESOURCES	Ahmad Zaki Yamani
MIN. OF PILGRIMAGE AFFAIRS & RELIGIOUS TRUSTS	Abd al-Wahhab Abd al-Wasi
MIN. OF PLANNING	Hisham Muhi al-Din Nazir
MIN. OF POSTS, TELEGRAPH & TELEPHONE	Dr. Alawi Darwish Kayyal
MIN. OF PUBLIC WORKS & HOUSING	Mit'ab bin Abd al-Aziz Al Saud
MINISTER OF STATE	Muhammad Ibrahim Masaud
MINISTER OF STATE	Dr. Abdallah Muhammad al-Umran
MINISTER OF STATE	Dr. Muhammad Abd al-Latif al-Mulham

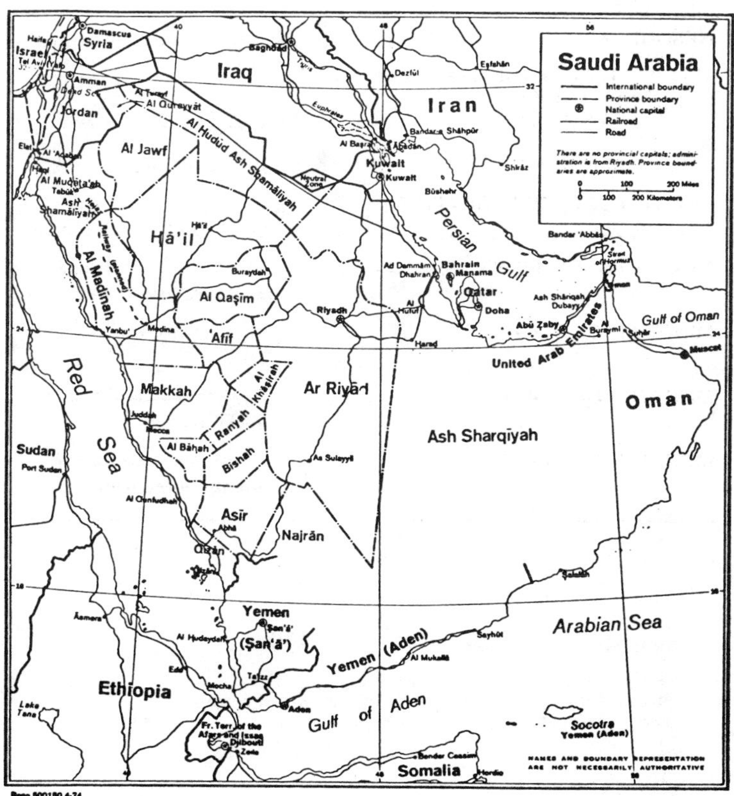

Base 500180 4-74

Take advantage of the special 20 percent discount on CSIS publications available only to *Washington Paper* subscribers!

If you subscribe to the *Washington Papers*, you are entitled to a special 20 percent discount on CSIS books, research monographs, and conference reports. In the quality tradition of the *Washington Papers*, these publications are available by mail from Georgetown University Center for Strategic and International Studies, 1800 K St., N.W., Washington, D.C. 20006. To qualify for the discount, you must include payment with your order and indicate that you are a *Washington Paper* subscriber. Please add 30c per publication for book-rate postage and handling.

	List Price	*Discount Price*
1. **World Power Assessment**, Ray S. Cline (1975); maps charts, tables, 173 pp.	$6.95	$5.55
2. **U.S./European Economic Cooperation in Military and Civil Technology**, Thomas A. Callaghan Jr. (1975); 126 pp.	$3.95	$3.15
3. **Foreign Policy Contingencies: The Next Five Years**, Edward Luttwak, Rapporteur (1975); 21 pp.	$1.95	$1.75
4. **Soviet Arms Aid in the Middle East**, Roger F. Pajak (1976); 45 pp.	$3.00	$2.60
5. **Communist Indochina: Problems, Policies and Superpower Involvement**, Joseph C. Kun (1976); 38 pp.	$3.00	$2.60
6. **Indonesia's Oil**, Sevinc Carlson (1976); maps, charts, tables, bibliography, 89 pp.	$3.95	$3.15
7. **A U.S. Guarantee for Israel?**, Mark A. Bruzonsky (1976); 62 pp.	$3.00	$2.60
8. **Armed Forces in the NATO Alliance**, Ulrich de Maiziere (1976); 48 pp.	$3.00	$2.60
9. **Europe, Japan, Canada, and the U.S.: The Interaction of Economic, Political, and Security Issues** (Third Quadrangular Conference), Edward Luttwak, Rapporteur (1976); 37 pp.	$3.95	$3.15
10. **The Political Stability of Italy**, Endre Marton, Rapporteur (1976); 67 pp.	$4.00	$3.20
11. **China Diary**, Harlan Cleveland (1976); 50 pp.	$3.00	$2.60
12. **The Soviet Union: Society and Policy** (Williamsburg Conference III), Endre Marton, Rapporteur (1976); 48 pp.	$3.00	$2.60
CSIS National Energy Seminar Reports, Francis C. Murray, Ed.		
13. **Deregulation of Natural Gas** (1976); 57 pp.	$3.00	$2.60
14. **The Energy Independence Authority** (1976); 56 pp.	$3.00	$2.60
15. **Divestiture: The Pros and Cons** (1976); 68 pp.	$3.00	$2.60